**MIMESIS
INTERNATIONAL**

AESTHETICS
n. 7

ADORNO AND POPULAR MUSIC

A Constellation of Perspectives

EDITED BY
COLIN J. CAMPBELL, SAMIR GANDESHA
AND STEFANO MARINO

© 2019 – MIMESIS INTERNATIONAL (Milano – Udine)
www.mimesisinternational.com
e-mail: info@mimesisinternational.com

Book series: *Aesthetics*, n. 7

Isbn: 9788869772238

© MIM Edizioni Srl
P.I. C.F. 02419370305

TABLE OF CONTENTS

INTRODUCTION 7
Colin J. Campbell, Samir Gandesha and Stefano Marino

"ANGELA DAVIS AS A COMMODITY?": ON THE COMMODITY
CHARACTER OF POPULAR MUSIC AND NEVERTHELESS
ITS TRUTH CONTENT 23
Stefano Marino

MINIMALISM AND RAVE MUSIC THROUGH ADORNO:
REPETITION AND ETERNAL RETURN OF THE SAME
IN CONTEMPORARY MUSIC 65
Alessandro Alfieri

THEODOR W. ADORNO DEFENDER OF POP MUSIC, *MALGRÉ LUI* 81
Giacomo Fronzi

CARRY MY BODY: "PROFANE REDEMPTION" AND FUGAZI 105
Colin J. Campbell

THE UNBEARABLE LIGHTNESS OF MUSIC? ADORNO'S CRITIQUE
OF THE MUSIC INDUSTRY 123
Marco Maurizi

Colin J. Campbell, Samir Gandesha
and Stefano Marino
INTRODUCTION

As is well-known, this year is an "Adornian" year: namely, it is the 50th anniversary of Theodor W. Adorno's untimely death on August 6, 1969 – exactly one month after King Crimson's famous debut performance at the free concert in Hyde Park with The Rolling Stones as headliners on July 5, 1969, and only a few days before the legendary music festival of Woodstock, held August 15-18, 1969, which attracted an unprecedentedly wide audience of thousands of people and at many levels forever changed the world of popular music. Adorno never witnessed the latter's impact on contemporary culture and the role of pop-rock music in the collective imaginary[1]. Yet it is the firm conviction of all participants in this volume, as authors and editors, that Adorno's intellectual legacy is still alive today, is more relevant than ever, and indeed a crucial resource of conceptual tools to develop a critical and active (rather than affirmative and passive) understanding of, and relationship with, the real at all levels. Furthermore, we are firmly convinced that, in the vast and complex corpus of Adorno's entire philosophical *oeuvre*, his aesthetic theory is most important and therefore deserves close and renewed attention today, for the constellation of perspectives it offers us in order to critically understand and transform the world we live in, instead of passively adapting and conforming ourselves to it.

We believe that, in turn, within the broad and articulated field of Adorno's philosophical meditations on art and on "the aesthetic"

---

[1] On 1969, the year in which Adorno died, as a fundamental year for the history of popular music, see Bertoncelli 2019.

as such[2], his (and Horkheimer's) conception of the culture industry is particularly worth examining today for the incomparable source of inspiration that it can provide to investigating current phenomena of aestheticization in the contemporary society of spectacle, of "atmospheres" and of aesthetic capitalism[3]. This is especially the case when one considers the role of the culture industry, particularly now in its digital form, in the return of the authoritarianism that so concerned Adorno in the post-war period[4]. If, as has been noted, it is "no exaggeration to say that crafting a theory to fit avant-garde artworks [...] has been the major preoccupation of art theorists in the 20th century", it is probably also no exaggeration to say that "attempting to accommodate mass-art forms" (which surely include popular music as well) "[is] the next major preoccupation of theories of art"[5]. Popular art in general, and popular music in particular, should be understood as central phenomena for contemporary aesthetics to address, due to their leading role and great influence in shaping our *sensus communis aestheticus*, and also due to their role in compelling us to broaden and rethink a part of the vocabulary and conceptuality of aesthetics as a philosophical discipline with regard to current aesthetic (or "aestheticized") practices and experiences and even "aesthetic mind"[6]. In Richard Shusterman's words, "popular art deserves serious aesthetic attention", and thus deserves to be defended from the attacks coming from a "powerful coalition of thinkers" vilifying it "as mindless, tasteless trash. The denigration of popular art or mass culture [is] particularly compelling since it is widely endorsed by intellectuals of violently different socio-political views and agendas"[7].

---

[2] For an interpretation that differentiates, within Adorno's philosophy, the aesthetic question concerning art (and autonomous art, in particular) and the aesthetic question concerning "the aesthetic" as such, i.e. as fundamental element of experience and of philosophizing connected to the non-identical understood as the non-conceptual, see Matteucci 2012 (pp. 97-172) and 2017.

[3] On this topic, see Gandesha and Hartle 2017, pp. X-LVIII.

[4] See Adorno 2019.

[5] Fisher 2005, p. 539.

[6] See Matteucci 2018a (in particular, pp. 5-22) and 2018b.

[7] Shusterman 2000, p. 169.

At the same time, critique is often overshadowed by an equally or more compelling celebration of popular culture in its form as a spectacle of commodities. Sometimes pop, too, must be defended against its devotees. In our view, Adorno's contributions to theorizing the reification and commodification of culture and the fetish-character in music, explicitly inspired by Marx's theorization of use value/exchange value and on the peculiar "sensuous supra-sensuous" constitution of the commodity form[8], can still prove to be very important and useful today to conceptually penetrate the pattern of the cultural industry: the increasing commodification of everyday life and of art, both serious and popular, and the idea of the "end" or "death" of art, connected with the gradual "anesthetization" of artworks after pop art, conceptual art and performance art, understandable as the logical/illogical counterpart of the abovementioned growing "aestheticization" of our everydayness that to a great extent characterizes our current way of making aesthetic experiences[9]. An Adornian approach to these and other related questions can show that, although sometimes viewed as radically different and sharply separated, they are essentially (and even dialectically) interrelated. As Adorno writes in a letter to Benjamin dated March 18, 1936, "high" and "low" culture are "torn halves of an integral freedom, to which however, they do not add up"[10]. And such an approach can thus pave the way for a philosophical aesthetics better able to orient us more critically to the "damaged life" of late capitalist society, especially with regard to the question concerning how the aesthetic form relates with the commodity form today.

Indeed, adopting an Adornian perspective, it appears clear that these questions cannot be answered on the basis of purely "aesthetic" considerations (as it sometimes happens in analytic

---

[8] On Adorno's use of the Marxian categories of alienation, commodity and fetishism for a critical understanding of contemporary music, in general, and of popular music, in particular, see GS 14, pp. 14-50 (Adorno 1991, pp. 29-60), GS 17, pp. 74-108 (Adorno 2002b, pp. 470-495), GS 18, pp. 729-777 (Adorno 2002b, pp. 391-436) and Adorno 2006a, pp. 271-326.

[9] In Arthur C. Danto's words, after Warhol's *Brillo Box* "if you were going to find out what art was, you had to turn from sense experience to thought" (Danto 1997, p. 13). Stefano Marino would like to thank Rolando Vitali for this suggestion.

[10] Adorno and Benjamin 1999, p. 130.

aesthetics, for example) precisely because of the socio-economic character of the art or cultural object that we aim to understand. If this is the case, then only a comprehensive, interdisciplinary critical theory, oriented toward grasping the "sensuous suprasensuous" constitution of its objects as a totality, can also prove to be able to understand the specific meaning of the aesthetic in our social, cultural and political reality. At the same time, we are firmly convinced that a rigorous critical theorist like Adorno deserves (and actually invites, by the very nature of his philosophy) critical attention and study, rather than an acritical and apologetic kind (as has sometimes been the case, in our opinion, in the studies of other great 20th-century philosophers, like Heidegger for example). We feel that Adorno would agree with Nietzsche's dictum that "[o]ne repays one's teacher badly by remaining a pupil"[11]. For this reason, all investigations of Adorno's concepts and works previously published by all contributors to this volume have always been animated by a genuine spirit of critical philosophizing, and thus have often proceeded dialectically "with Adorno" and simultaneously "against Adorno". This is precisely the critical and, as it were, negative-dialectical style that we also aim to adopt in this volume, convinced as we are that only an approach of this kind can do justice to the richness, complexity and, again, critical nature of Adorno's philosophizing.

With his seminal works on the culture industry, film and especially popular music, Adorno was one of the most important and rigorous theorists of the aesthetics of popular arts in the twentieth century. At the same time, however, he seemingly denied any legitimacy and "truth content" to them, especially to jazz and popular music (his favorite examples of "pseudo-culture" from the early 1930s until the late 1960s). This can sometimes make his conception appear "hard to digest" (exactly in contrast to popular music that, for him, was completely "pre-digested") or even as "indefensible"[12], given the general rethinking, reconsideration and reconceptualization that, for example, the relationship between so-called "high art" and "low art" (which also includes the relationship between "serious music" and "popular music",

---

11   Nietzsche 2003, p. 59.
12   Leppert 2002, p. 356.

to use Adorno's own terms[13]) has undergone from the 1960s until today, with a veritable paradigm shift in comparison to the "heroic period" of the 1910s/1920s (to still use an expression frequently used by Adorno). Limiting ourselves to just one example, an outstanding critical theorist of our time, Mark Fisher, decided to open his influential manifesto *Capitalist Realism* by referring to a movie as a symbol of our critical epoch (Alfonso Cuarón's 2006 film *Children of Men*), with specific reference to "one of [its] key scenes" in which are shown "cultural treasures [...] preserved in a building that is itself a refurbished heritage artifact" that include "Michelangelo's *David*, Picasso's *Guernica*, Pink Floyd's inflatable pig"[14] – thus implicitly considering as acceptable the mix of Renaissance art, early twentieth-century avant-garde art and popular music/popular culture under the common concept of "cultural treasures". This fact evidently marks something like a paradigm shift in comparison to Adorno's apparent view of *all* mass culture as "pseudo-culture" or mere administration and hence not culture in the strict sense. It is not by chance that Adorno's first and perhaps most important collection of essays on cultural criticism and society, namely *Prisms* from 1955, also included his last contribution explicitly focused on the untrue character of jazz, namely the essay "Perennial Fashion – Jazz", beside essays on cultural and social phenomena provided for him by a relevant truth content like Bach, Schönberg, Valéry, Benjamin or Kafka. The abovementioned impression of a veritable paradigm shift in cultural criticism with regard to popular culture can be obviously connected, among other things, to the impact in the last decades of research on subcultures etc. in the field of cultural studies, and is reinforced when Fisher in *Capitalist Realism* (still using the Adorno/Fisher comparison for our purposes) precisely chooses an example taken from the field of popular music, namely Kurt Cobain and his band Nirvana (and not Schönberg or Berg as "dialectical composers" and symbols of progress in music, as Adorno would have done) to exemplify the idea of the residual chances of artistic protest against the system of reified and commodified mainstream culture:

---

13 Adorno 2006a, pp. 280-284.
14 Fisher 2009, p. 1.

What we are dealing with now is not the incorporation of materials that previously seemed to possess subversive potentials, but instead, their *pre-corporation*: the pre-emptive formatting and shaping of desires, aspirations and hopes by capitalist culture. [...] "Alternative" and "independent" don't designate [today] something outside mainstream culture; rather, they are styles, in fact *the* dominant styles, within the mainstream. No-one embodied (and struggled with) this deadlock more than Kurt Cobain and Nirvana. In his dreadful lassitude and objectless rage, Cobain seemed to give wearied voice to the despondency of the generation that had come after history, whose every move was anticipated, tracked, bought and sold before it had even happened. Cobain knew that he was just another piece of spectacle, that nothing runs better on MTV than a protest against MTV; knew that his every move was a cliché scripted in advance, knew that even realizing it is a cliché. [...] Cobain found himself in "a world in which stylistic innovation is no longer possible, [where] all that is left is to imitate dead styles, to speak through the masks and with the voices of the styles in the imaginary museum". Here, even success meant failure, since to succeed would only mean that you were the new meat on which the system could feed. But the high existential angst of Nirvana and Cobain belongs to an older moment; what succeeded them was a pastiche-rock which reproduced the forms of the past without anxiety. Cobain's death confirmed the defeat and incorporation of rock's utopian and promethean ambitions.[15]

In a sense, Fisher's comments on the post-Cobain situation in contemporary music could have been endorsed by Adorno, but probably with reference to the post-Schönberg situation in serious music (arguing, for example, that after the incorporation in now harmless pseudo-avant-garde music of "materials that previously seemed to possess subversive potentials", after "the high existential angst" of *Erwartung* and *Pierrot Lunaire*, after the hope that atonal music "could change anything" etc., it seemed as if "every move was anticipated, tracked, bought and sold before it had even happened"[16]) and surely not with reference to popular music

---

15   Fisher 2009, pp. 9-10.
16   It can be interesting to compare Fisher's reference to "the high existential angst of Nirvana and Cobain" to Adorno's reference to "the terror which Schoenberg and Webern spread", to "their music [which] gives form

that, for him, was always and only a form of "social cement"[17], a commodity in the strict sense produced and commercialized in order to strengthen the already existing order of "a society of commodities"[18]. For Adorno, "perhaps a better hour may at some time strike"; however, "not popular music but artistic music has furnished a model for [the] possibility" that "art, in unity with the society, [may] ever leave the road of the always-identical"[19]. As he observes a propos of the (for him) unavoidable and insurmountable commodity character of *all* popular music:

> We live in a society of commodities – that is, a society in which production of goods is taking place, not primarily to satisfy human wants and needs, but for profit. Human needs are satisfied only incidentally, as it were. This basic condition of production affects the form of the product as well as the human interrelationships. [...] In our commodity society there exists a general trend toward a heavy concentration of capital which makes for a shrinking of the free market in favor of monopolized mass production of standardized goods; this holds true particularly of the communications industry. [...] Whereas on the one hand standardization necessarily follows from the conditions of contemporary economy, it becomes, on the other hand, one of the means of preserving [the] commodity society [...]. What seems significant [...] in the present situation, and what is certainly deeply connected with the trend to standardization and mass production, is that *today the commodity character of*

---

to that anxiety, that terror, that insight into the catastrophic situation which others merely evade by regressing" (GS 14, p. 50 [Adorno 1991, p. 60]). On angst and loneliness as the emotional and expressive content of Schönberg's "radical music", see also GS 12, pp. 42-51 (Adorno 2006b, pp. 34-41). On Cobain's unprecedented significance in the contemporary musical scene, see also the jazz pianist Brad Mehldau's fitting and to some extent also moving observations in the booklet of his 4-CD box *Ten Years Solo Live* (in which he also offers an incredibly intense solo piano version of Nirvana's hit "Smells Like Teen Spirit"): "Kurt Cobain, with his lyrics and way of singing, inadvertently become a spokesperson for my generation. That music spoke to the way we all felt lost and untethered in the world. [...] Kurt Cobain had that 'for-real' vulnerability, and it seemed he had no choice but to scream it out at us, completely unhinged, like a scared manchild. That's what made his expression so strong".

17 Adorno 2006a, pp. 315-319.
18 Adorno 2006a, p. 135.
19 GS 14, p. 49 (Adorno 1991, p. 59).

> music tends radically to alter it. [...] That is to say, music has ceased to be a human force and is consumed like other consumer goods. This produces "commodity listening", a listening whose ideal it is to dispense as far as possible with any effort on the part of the recipient.[20]

So, returning to the specific meaning and scope of this book, our idea is that, in recognizing the invaluable significance and actuality of Adorno's philosophical-sociological-musicological theory of both serious and popular music, one must always try not to adopt an orthodox (and thus acritical) Adornian perspective but rather an unorthodox (and thus critical) approach towards Adorno himself. Of course, this is *not* meant here, i.e. in this volume, as a sterile exercise of distinguishing between what is living and what is dead in Adorno 50 years after his death – an approach strongly criticized by Adorno himself, by the way, in his own interpretation of Hegel 125 years after his death, inasmuch as he wrote:

> A historical occasion like the 125th anniversary of Hegel's death could have elicited what we call an "appreciation". But that concept has become untenable, if indeed it ever had any value. It makes the impudent claim that because one has the dubious good fortune to live later, and because one has a professional interest in the person one is to talk about, one can sovereignly assign the dead person his place, thereby in some sense elevating oneself above him. This arrogance echoes in the loathsome question of what in Kant, and now Hegel as well, has any meaning for the present – and even the so-called Hegel renaissance began half a century ago with a book by Benedetto Croce that undertook to distinguish between what was living and what was dead in Hegel. The converse question is not even raised: what the present means in the face of Hegel.[21]

Rather, what has been just said above about adopting a critical instead than an acritical and purely celebrative approach is meant in this volume as an exercise of critical rethinking and revitalization of his theories in light of current developments in the main fields of application of his theories, like popular culture and popular

---

20 Adorno 2006a, pp. 135-137.
21 GS 5, p. 251 (Adorno 1993, p. 1).

music. As noted by Richard Middleton, Adorno's general position "opened up new ground, in ways which often remain of value", but at the same time "his specific treatment of the social situation of popular music, by proceeding, in his usual way, 'through the extremes', does have the negative virtue of exaggerating real trends. Anyone wanting to argue the importance of studying popular music has to absorb Adorno in order to go beyond him"[22].

On the basis of these and other fundamental presuppositions that will be clarified and made explicit in the single chapters, the authors of the contributions collected in this book will attempt to fulfill the aim of taking Adorno's philosophy of music absolutely seriously and to try to critically rethink it when this is required. In fact, as noted by Richard Leppert, "Adorno's contribution to popular music research is unimpeachable, despite the fact that he [...] held strong prejudices, didn't know a fraction of a repertory he attacked, and didn't change his mind (very much or often) on the topic [...]. The small obsession with Adorno on the part of the popular-culture scholars is a tacit, if sometimes inadvertent, acknowledgment not only of the vitality of his ideas but also of the pervasiveness of the social and cultural conditions that produced his account in the first place"[23]. We feel that Adorno's critique of popular music has shown itself to be unerringly true in general, and until society has been emancipated it will most likely continue to be true and to resonate with a variety of other Marxist and non-Marxist schools of criticism. However, we are obliged to add that to obscure the particular by overemphasizing the general is a cardinal mistake (no simple error!) in non-systemic negative dialectics. The content of this volume therefore arises out of the tension between the general trend and specific "moments" (to invoke Lester Bangs[24]), decisive acts of musical resistance and reclamation of the human potential that is decimated by commodification and continuous economic expansion.

So, "simply stated, [...] Adorno heard right", but at the same time we must admit that sometimes "he [also] heard wrong"[25].

---

22   Middleton 1990, p. 35.
23   Leppert 2002, p. 348.
24   Bangs 1987, p. 298.
25   Leppert 2002, pp. 347-348.

Like perhaps no other music theorist of the twentieth century, Adorno has offered us essential intuitions, insights and conceptualizations to critically understand the adventures and misadventures of contemporary music, and also interpretative schemes that, although originally coined and conceived of for serious music, in some cases may be fruitfully applied to popular music and help us discover new dimensions of it that had previously passed unnoticed. A good example, in this sense, would be Perry Anderson's original (though not entirely unproblematic) application of Adorno's interpretation scheme of the polarized situation of twentieth-century serious music as divided between Schönberg and Stravinsky ("for only in the extremes does the essence of this music take shape distinctively; only they permit knowledge of its truth content[26]) to the situation of rock music as divided between the extremes of The Beatles and The Rolling Stones. As Anderson observed:

> It is incorrect to say that the Stones are "not major innovators". Perhaps a polarization Stones/Beatles such as Adorno constructed between Schoenberg and Stravinsky (evoked by Beckett) might actually be a fruitful exercise. Suffice it to say here that, for all their intelligence and refinement, the Beatles have never strayed much beyond the strict limits of romantic convention: central moments of their oeuvre are nostalgia and whimsy, both eminently consecrated traditions of middle-class England. Lukács's pejorative category of the *Angenehme* – the "pleasant" which dulls and pacifies – fits much of their work with deadly accuracy. By contrast, the Stones have refused the given orthodoxy of pop music; their work is a dark and veridical negation of it. It is an astonishing fact that there is virtually not one Jagger-Richards composition which is conventionally about a "happy" or "unhappy" personal relationship. Love, jealousy and lament – the substance of 85 per cent of traditional pop music – are missing. Sexual exploitation, mental disintegration and physical immersion are their substitutes.[27]

Now, Anderson's critical assessment of The Beatles' supposed "pleasant" and "pacified" (i.e., in Marcusian terms, "affirmative")

---

26 GS 12, p. 13 (Adorno 2006b, p. 7).
27 Perry Anderson, quoted in Cummings 2013.

music can be easily judged as expressing a far too general, superficial and unfair evaluation of the "Fab Four"[28]. However, it must be also said that such a use of Adornian categories (the Schönberg/Stravinskij polarization in the *Philosophy of New Music*) in order to decipher certain phenomena of contemporary popular music in terms of negation, disintegration, truth content and protest, namely in terms of a critique of the administered world and its alienation and commodification, reveals some potentialities that are present in Adorno's writings, ones that require a combination of philological exactness, on the one hand, and originality and fantasy in interpretation, on the other hand, to be discovered and then developed.

The contributions collected in this volume – written by expert scholars of both Adorno's philosophy of music and musicology in general such as Alessandro Alfieri, Giacomo Fronzi and Marco Maurizi, along with the editors of the book – try to do justice to the unprecedented breadth and richness of Adorno's philosophy of music (limiting our attention in this book on his theory of popular music). In order to accomplish this aim, in planning and then realizing this book we thought that what is required is a constellation of different perspectives aimed not at abandoning a critical understanding of popular music but rather at improving it and further developing it beyond Adorno's own intentions and, as it were, his limitations. As the readers of the present book will see, the collection is not only understood by its authors and editors to be a constellation of different approaches and points of view on the subject at issue (without prejudice to the unitary character of our respective investigations that is guaranteed by our common and constant reference to the tradition and philosophical framework of critical theory) but also as a constellation of different musical phenomena of our time that range from minimalism and techno/rave music to politically committed rock songs of the 1960s/1970s and "experimental" rock music of various kinds (psychedelia, progressive, noise) up to punk, hardcore, grunge, crossover and nu metal. As Adorno famously writes at the beginning of the

---

28 Lemmy Kilmister, among others, would have said so emphatically, as he did in his discussion of the Beatles and the Stones in the 2010 film *Lemmy* (dirs. Orshoski, Olliver).

"Paralipomena" section of *Aesthetic Theory*, "philosophy [...] is nothing but the thought that refuses all restrictions"[29]. Struggling to be dialectically faithful to Adorno and at the same time faithful to our own diverse experiences of music, within the limits of our capacities (which, of course, are not comparable to those of Adorno, convinced as we are that he was "the greatest philosopher of music of the twentieth century"[30]) in this book we have tried to refuse all prejudicial restrictions concerning popular music, including those that could be derived from Adorno himself, and to inquire into it from the perspective of critical theory with the hope of offering new and original contributions on the 50th anniversary of his death.

The various contributions included in the present collection focus on different moments of Adorno's philosophy of music in general, and his theory of popular music in particular, also adopting different perspectives and sometimes differing from each other because of diverse nuances and emphasis on some aspects. But all the authors included in this book share the same interest both in Adorno and in popular music, and above all share the same aim to preserve the critique of the commodity while sometimes tracing the way an Adornian commodity critique of music can overstep itself. One of the possible implications of this perspective and approach (explicitly stated in some chapters and only implicit in others) is that Adorno himself and his theory could be, indeed have been, commodified. Adorno himself knew that this could happen, as he wrote in his late masterpiece *Negative Dialectics*: "no theory today escapes the marketplace"[31]. Thus, in a sense, from our critical perspective both popular and "elite" forms (such as academic German critical theory or "serious" music) require something like the same kind of "rescue" from commodity-oblivion, and our different readings of Adorno in this book aim to de-commodify him from within, as it were.

From the common perspective of the authors of this book what is needed from popular music to escape commodification is that it, much like philosophy, must become "ruthlessly self-critical", where

---

29 GS 7, p. 391 (Adorno 2002a, p. 262).
30 Matassi 2004, p. 89.
31 Adorno 1990, p. 4.

by "self-critical" we do not mean "self-righteous" but rather "self-reflective". If this is the case, then it can be said that ruthlessly self-reflective songs, songs that induce (because of their form and/or their content) the listeners to reflect on themselves as listeners of commodity music, to reflect on that experience – that such songs can "succeed by failing", as it were. Among the many and very different examples that could be mentioned here (given also the great diversity and variety of the broad and complex universe of contemporary popular music) we would limit ourselves to invite the reader to think of certain songs from Lou Reed, David Bowie, Peter Gabriel, Radiohead and still others that may be understood as tragic songs in the sense that they dramatize the isolation and loneliness of the musician and the audience alike in a commodity world.

In this regard, it is surely important to note what many critics (sometimes with a highly nuanced position, but sometimes not) have called Adorno's "authoritarianism" and his sense of a quasi-teleological "determinism" in music history, and to pay adequately attention to it, but at the same time not to overemphasize and overstate it. In a sense, it could be said indeed that one of the problems Adorno had with popular music was due to the passion that music induces. As many commentators have observed, especially with regard to his critique of jazz, Adorno was sometimes arbitrary in his preferences, but perhaps many critics can only take that arbitrariness as authoritarian rage, and cannot perceive the human-ness in it. So, one of the aims of the present collection is that of de-commodifying also Adorno's philosophy of music and to render him as a person, as a limited, finite person who had only his own experiences and his own 'loves to love' (to invoke Lester Bangs' writing on Van Morrison). This is especially true of his monographs on Mahler and Berg, his true musical heroes, and also (shifting our attention from music to literature) the anecdote of the eighteen-years-old Adorno accidentally meeting Thomas Mann, "a writer [that] ever since his youth Adorno had felt great admiration for", and "walk[ing] behind him, imagining what he might say to him"[32], like a young fan of Bono or Bruce Springsteen or Eddie Vedder might do with his/her pop-rock musical hero these days.

---

32   Müller-Doohm 2005, pp. 314-315.

The challenge of music criticism, and of philosophizing "on" music (or, in Adorno's particular case, philosophizing "with" music and even "in" music), is thus to do justice to self-reflection, to really reflect our own idiosyncratic experiences, without wishing away the universal commodity form. If applied to the task of a critical interpretation and updated actualization of Adorno's seminal theories on popular music, rather than simply "trimming down" Adorno, as many critics appear to do, we could more charitably acknowledge (beside the great, indeed unprecedented strength of many of his concepts) his weakness, which is the necessary weakness of anyone who dares to publish anything "true" about an experience as profound and complex as that of music. Among other things, what is important for us, as much from critical theory as from the pop-rock music we appreciate and love, is to present Adorno to the reader as a person who did not have the only or final opinion on music, who saw remarkable and deeply meaningful structures in music we can still learn from, but did not know the future. As Adorno observes in *Negative Dialectics*, "the pedantries of all systems [...] are the marks of an a priori inescapable failure, noted with incomparable honesty in the fractures of the Kantian system"[33]. It is our conviction that this also applies to Adorno, who notoriously defined his own original version of dialectical philosophy as "an anti-system"[34], and that especially in the case of his theory of popular music what we may call its fractures and sometimes even its deficiencies testify "with incomparable honesty" its greatness and ongoing fruitfulness to critically understanding popular music today.

Bibliography

Adorno Th. W.
1970 ff. *Gesammelte Schriften* (quoted as GS), ed. by R. Tiedemann, Suhrkamp, Frankfurt a.M.
1991. *The Culture Industry: Selected Essays on Mass Culture*, ed. by J.M. Bernstein, Routledge, London.

---

33 Adorno 1990, pp. 21-22.
34 Adorno 1990, p. XX.

1993. *Hegel. Three Studies*, trans. by S. Weber Nicholsen, The MIT Press, London-Cambridge (MA).
2002a. *Aesthetic Theory*, trans. by R. Hullot-Kentor, Continuum, London-New York.
2002b. *Essays on Music*, trans. by S.H. Gillespie et al., ed. by R.D. Leppert, The University of California Press, Berkeley.
2006a. *Current of Music. Elements of a Radio Theory*, ed. by R. Hullot-Kentor, Polity Press, Cambridge-Malden (MA).
2006b. *Philosophy of New Music*, trans. and ed. by R. Hullot-Kentor, University of Minnesota Press, Minneapolis-London.
2019. *Aspekte des neuen Rechtsradikalismus: Ein Vortrag*, Suhrkamp, Frankfurt a.M.

Adorno Th. W. and Benjamin W.
1999. *The Complete Correspondence: 1928-1940*, trans. by N. Walker, Harvard University Press, Cambridge (MA).

Bangs L.
1987. *Psychotic Reactions and Carburetor Dung: The Work of a Legendary Critic: Rock 'n' Roll as Literature and Literature as Rock 'n' Roll*, ed. by G. Marcus, Anchor Press, New York.

Bertoncelli R.
2019. *1969, da Abbey Road a Woodstock*, Giunti, Firenze.

Cummings J.
2013. "Perry Anderson Meets the Rolling Stones" (available at: https://chaosofmemories.wordpress.com/2013/02/19/perry-anderson-meets-the-rolling-stones; last accessed: August 13, 2019).

Danto A.C.
1997. *After the End of Art: Contemporary Art and the Pale of History*, Princeton University Press, Princeton.

Fisher J.A.
2005. "High Art Versus Low Art", in B. Gaut and D. McIver Lopes (ed.), *The Routledge Companion to Aesthetics* (2nd edition), Routledge, London-New York, pp. 527-540.

Fisher M.
2009. *Capitalist Realism: Is There No Alternative?*, O Books, Winchester-Washington.

Gandesha S. and Hartle J.F. (eds.)
2017. *Aesthetic Marx*, Bloomsbury, London-New York.

Leppert R.
2002. "Introduction" and "Commentary" to Th. W. Adorno, *Essays on Music*, trans. by S.H. Gillespie et al., ed. by R.D. Leppert, The University of California Press, Berkeley.

Matassi E.
2004. *Musica*, Guida, Napoli.

Matteucci G.
2012. *L'artificio estetico. Moda e bello naturale in Simmel e Adorno*, Mimesis, Milano-Udine.
2017. "Adorno's Aesthetic Constellation from Shudder to Fashion: A Form of Life in the Age of Globalization?", in "Zeitschrift für Ästhetik und Allgemeine Kunstwissenschaft", vol. 62, n. 1, pp. 41-55.
2018a. *Elementi per un'estetica del contemporaneo*, Bononia University Press, Bologna.
2018b. "The (Aesthetic) Extended Mind: Aesthetics from Experience-Of to Experience-With", in C. Vaughan and I. Vidmar (ed.), *Proceedings of the European Society for Aesthetics*, vol. 10, pp. 400-429.

Mehldau B.
2015. "Liner Notes" to *Ten Years Solo Live* (4 CD), Nonesuch Records.

Middleton R.
1990. *Studying Popular Music*, Open University Press, Milton Keynes-Philadelphia.

Müller-Doohm S.
2005. *Adorno: A Biography*, Polity Press, Cambridge-Malden (MA).

Nietzsche F.W.
2003. *Thus Spake Zarathustra*, trans. by T. Wayne, Algora, New York.

Stefano Marino

"ANGELA DAVIS AS A COMMODITY?"
On the Commodity Character of Popular Music and Nevertheless its Truth Content[*]

For Giovanni Matteucci,
with gratitude for his constant support
during all these years.

In some of my previous contributions I have tried to develop a sort of partial critical rethinking of Adorno's aesthetics of popular music by focusing on the songs on the genocide of the Armenian people written by the heavy metal band System Of A Down (in my paper "Writing Songs after Auschwitz"[1]), and then by comparing Adorno's and Shusterman's approaches to questions concerning popular music (in my paper "A Somaesthetic Approach to Rock Music"[2]). And in my previous book *La filosofia di Frank Zappa. Un'interpretazione adorniana* I have tried to develop an analogous enterprise by specifically comparing Adorno's aesthetics and the

---

[*] A first version of this work was presented at a thematic panel on the culture industry that I organized and supervised in the context of the 12th International Critical Theory Conference in Roma (May 9-11, 2019). I would like to thank the organizers of the conference for having invited me and all the participants to the thematic panel (both the other speakers of the panel, Mario Farina and Gioia Laura Iannilli, and the people in the audience, especially Hugh Miller) for their questions and suggestions that greatly helped me to improve my investigation of this topic in view of its publication.

[1] The paper was first presented at the conference "Global Adorno" in Amsterdam in March 2016, and then published both in a shorter version in English and in a longer version in Italian (see Marino 2017a and 2017b).

[2] The paper was first presented at the conference "The Soma as the Core of Aesthetics, Ethics and Politics" at the University of Szeged, and then published (see Marino 2018).

poetics of a rock musician *sui generis* like Frank Zappa[3]. In the present contribution I will try to exemplify my ideas on Adorno and popular music in an even more concrete and more effective form, and to potentially further develop them, by focusing on a different but nevertheless closely related example. Namely: the example of politically committed pop-rock songs (where the concept of *commitment*, as is well-known, also plays an important role in Adorno's aesthetics[4]), and more specifically the popular music song-hits composed and performed in the early 1970s in support of Angela Davis. These songs were explicitly written for a critical theorist, a pupil of Marcuse, who had also studied for some time in Germany with Adorno (who eventually wrote a very positive *Gutachten* for her[5]). As Davis herself recalls in her autobiography:

> My decision to study in Frankfurt had been made in 1964, against the backdrop of a relative political tranquility. But by the time I left in the summer of 1965, thousands of sisters and brothers were screaming in the streets of Los Angeles [...]. I was certain that Frankfurt was far more conducive to philosophical studies than any other place. But each day it was becoming clearer to me that my ability to accomplish anything was directly dependent on my ability to contribute to something concrete to the struggle. Adorno had readily agreed to direct my work on a doctoral dissertation. But now I felt it would be impossible for me to stay in Germany any longer. Two years was enough. I arranged for an appointment with Adorno and explained to him that I had to go home. [...] I wanted to continue my academic work, but I knew I could not do it unless I was politically involved.[6]

---

3 See Marino 2014.
4 See, for example, GS 11, pp. 409-430 (Adorno 1992, pp. 76-94); and GS 7, pp. 365-368 (Adorno 2002a, pp. 246-248).
5 Adorno's recommendation letter for Davis can be viewed here: http://www.literaturarchiv1968.de/content/theodor-w-adornos-gutachten-fuer-angela-davis.
6 Davis 1988, pp. 143-145. As has been noted, "Angela Davis took a different message from Marcuse" in comparison to Adorno: "'Herbert Marcuse taught me that it was possible to be an academic, an activist, a scholar, and a revolutionary'", as she once declared. "[S]he studied with Marcuse in Brandeis and with Adorno in Frankfurt and then, in 1966 when the Black Panther Party was founded, she felt drawn back to the United States, in part, to work in radical movements. Adorno had been sceptical: 'He

The general question that I would like to ask and to discuss here by using this particular example is what happens, from an Adornian point of view, when a critical theorist, someone who is supposed to develop a critical theory and a critical praxis against the growing commodification of culture and life in the contemporary age, becomes him- or herself a commodity? That is, when he or she (e.g. the critical theorist) is used as the object or content of a commodified product (be it a puppet, a t-shirt, a comic book, a TV series or a rock song) produced and commercialized by the culture industry? Far from being purely theoretical or even merely rhetorical questions, these are indeed very concrete and actual problems, and there are plenty of real examples in this field that can be mentioned and referred to. Quite interestingly, such examples precisely range from t-shirts[7] and puppets[8] of Walter Benjamin, to new brands in the field of fast-fashion that even take their name from the name of critical theorists/feminists in order to spread and commercialize a view of the woman's role in society that may even appear quite at odds with critical theory and radical feminism[9], to comic strips of Herbert Marcuse (like his recent graphic biography, with a Foreword by Angela Davis, incidentally[10]), to rock songs written in favor and in support of Angela Davis. Choosing to focus here on this last example, due to my abovementioned long-lasting research interest in the aesthetics of popular music, and following a list provided by Wikipedia's entry on Davis, we may mention:

---

suggested that my desire to work directly in the radical movements of that period was akin to a media studies scholar deciding to become a radio technician'" (Jeffries 2017).

7   See: https://www.pinterest.it/pin/32228953554569604.
8   See: https://www.pinterest.it/pin/520729394114118562.
9   While writing this paper I discovered indeed a fast-fashion Italian brand that, although apparently not connected in any way with the real Angela Davis (or Angela Yvonne Davis, to mention her complete name), has been called *Angela Davis* and so described: "Angela Davis is an Italian apparel brand, it was born in the late '90s and immediately distinguished by its style and identity. Angela Davis will appeal to a dynamic and ultra-feminine woman, attentive to the latest fashion trends and the quality of the garments at affordable prices. Angela Davis is a revolutionary brand in the fast-fashion pay attention to the trends of the moment managing to capture and meet the demands of the changing market" (http://www.angeladavisfashion.it/En-Home/).
10 See Thorkelson 2019.

the song "Angela" written by the Italian singer and songwriter Virgilio Savona with his group Quartetto Cetra; the song "Sweet Black Angel", written by The Rolling Stones and released on their 1972 classic album *Exile on Main Street*; the song "George Jackson", written by Bob Dylan about the shooting of the Black Panthers' Leader and the events of the case that eventually led to Angela Davis' arrest and trial; the song "Canzone per Angela Davis" by the Italian group Canzoniere Internazionale; the song "Angela", written by John Lennon and released on his 1972 classic album with Yoko Ono *Some Time in New York City*.

So, once again, the question is: what happens when a critical theorist (like Angela Davis, in this case) becomes the object or content of "a mass commodity" characterized by a "standardized commodity character"[11] which "is actually factory-made through and through"[12] like, for Adorno, a "light popular music song-hit"[13]? Or, more in general, what happens when a critical theorist and a radical thinker becomes a pop icon and a pop idol? What are the aesthetic and at the same time socio-political consequences of situations and operations of this kind? The two levels, the aesthetic and the social, are tightly connected in the constellation of moments and dimensions that form Adorno's complex and multi-layered concept of the artwork's truth content. These questions, of course, can be also connected to the potential danger of "commodification" that other relevant figures of a broadly speaking leftist socio-cultural imaginary (like Che Guevara or Karl Marx himself) may undergo when they are used as subjects for works overall belonging to the culture industry, like blockbuster movies or TV series or pop-rock songs or gadgets of all kinds, or even as subjects for works of high art, inasmuch as the latter, after the different stages of development of aestheticization processes from the 1950s until today (in chronological order: pop art, postmodernism and widespread aesthetics[14]), has started to "flirt" quite often with forms, structures, paradigms, models and styles of low or popular art.

---

11   GS 17, p. 78 (Adorno 2002b, p. 473).
12   GS 10/1, p. 126 (Adorno 1997, p. 123).
13   Adorno 2006a, p. 277.
14   I follow Mecacci 2017 in this reconstruction and interpretation scheme of twentieth-century aestheticization processes and stages of development.

In this context, I would like to mention a question that I asked to the editors of the volume *Aesthetic Marx*, Samir Gandesha and Johan Hartle, in a forum of discussion on their book published in 2018 on the journal "Lebenswelt", where I observed:

> the fascinating and fitting formula "Aesthetic Marx" may seem to dangerously point in a broader and in-itself-articulated direction, namely in the direction of a sort of aestheticization and, connected to this, commodification of Marx himself. [...] What I refer to here is an aestheticization of Marx under the form of his transformation into an aesthetic object or content in works of art that, for their part, run the risk of being subject to strong commodification processes in our widely aestheticized age of "aesthetic capitalism". [...] The use of Marx in the visual arts (and one could perhaps add analogous examples in the popular arts: film, pop music, photography, etc.) is a relevant tendency of our age [...]. Now, according to some scholars it is possible to identify in today's so-called "aesthetic capitalism", and in "the artworld" that belongs to it, a certain trend to consciously and even happily turn artworks into commodities or even the visual arts into a form of business, for example with Warhol, Koons, Hirst and others [...]. Adorno famously wrote with his unique negative and prescriptive style that "the task of art today is to bring chaos into order", whereas such expressions as "Warhol economy" or "business art"[15], that have acquired a widespread diffusion and common use today, unmistakably reveal the opposite (affirmative-apologetic, rather than negative-critical) tendency to accommodate oneself to the world order as it is, without any intention to criticize it and transform it. On this basis, my questions are: (1) whether you think, on the one side, that using Marx as the image for commodified artworks might entail the commodification of Marx himself and hence the risk of assimilating or integrating him into the existing reality; and then (2) whether you think, on the other side, that Marx's and a Marx-inspired aesthetics can provide a contribution for a critical understanding of the abovementioned contemporary scenarios in art and aesthetics, also in this case as a counterbalance or countermovement to predominant trends in the

---

For a general overview on aestheticization, see Iannilli 2018; for a more theoretical interpretation of this phenomenon, see Matteucci 2016 and 2017.

15 I borrow the concept of "Warhol economy" from Church Gibson 2012.

philosophy of art our time that rather tends to be merely descriptive and thus uncritical.[16]

Gandesha's and Hartle's long and detailed answer to my question (which I allow myself to mention here because it can provide useful elements also to reflect on the example of the use of the image and figure of Angela Davis in popular music) was:

> The danger of aestheticization of leftist politics is real: especially since leftist theory in general has often found its refuge in the cultural field – to then being attacked by right wing populist that it is elitist and unreal. In fact, [...] this aesthetic or artistic leftism is very much aporetic but this aporia is the very aporia of autonomous art, itself: that it promises an alternative world while merely compensating the flaws of the really existing one. This has been the Adornian argument ever since: aesthetic autonomy is both necessary and an ideology. It seems that in contemporary art Marx is quite often being referred to as the personification of this contradiction. On the international art biennials, it seems, you see more references to Marx and to the critique of political economy than in contemporary debates in the social sciences. And what is so uncomfortable about this is that the fact that such debates happen in the restricted realm of artistic discourse and cultural representation might, as a form of compensation, end up consolidating its shortcomings in manifest political struggles. Such dangers of aestheticization are quite concrete in the reception of the work of Jacques Rancière [...]. The problem seems to begin at the moment at which such theories are incorporated into the art world and start being interpreted as a justification of the primacy of aesthetic politics, that is, of a form of politics that focuses primarily on aesthetic practices and implicitly justifies and legitimizes a social structure that is predetermined by the field specific logics of art with its specific class composition. This becomes its blind-spot, as it were. [...] Will Marx end up being a merely artsy Marx in some cultural milieu? This question very much depends if Marx could possibly be separated from the logics of capital and class warfare. We don't see this risk, yet. Rather, art practices, because of the specific logics of the field that bind art to universal promises, on the one hand [...] and to a continuous self-reflection of the conditions under which they operate [...], are a

---

16   Marino, in Farina and Marino 2018, pp. 6-7.

refuge to certain types of critical discourse, on the other. Therefore, the aestheticization of Marx provides a refuge to leftist politics in the field of ideology (or "ideological state apparatuses"), in a conjuncture that leaves precious little space for Marxism in the more direct, and in some ways more real, realm of political economy, and practical politics. [...] The ideology of the aesthetic (Eagleton) must not be underestimated and symbolic politics, politics of representation and semiotic revolts, must not be mistaken for politics *in toto*. But, as also Eagleton points out, Aesthetic discourse and the art field are also sublimations of political desires for emancipation that find little possibilities for expression where they belong.[17]

I think that, following what I will call here an *orthodox* Adornian approach to the aesthetics of popular music, we should say that (1) it is wrong to use a critical theorist as the object or content of a popular music song-hit: namely, of a work that, as such, for Adorno is only "a commodity in the strict sense"[18] and strengthens the almighty alienation-, reification- and commodification-power of the culture industry, using the name or image of a critical theorist for acritical and indeed ideological purposes. This is an idea that we can find clearly expressed in Adorno's early and best-known contributions on this topic from the 1930s/1940s, such as his essays on jazz and popular music and the famous chapter of *Dialectic of Enlightenment* on the culture industry, and that – with very few exceptions – he kept unchanged until the 1960s, as expressed for example by the chapter on popular music in his 1962 *Introduction to the Sociology of Music*[19], by his 1963 résumé on the culture industry[20], by his decision to republish in 1964 without changes his essay *On Jazz* from 1936 (thus confirming to still adhere to that interpretation of jazz after many decades[21]), or also from the following passage from his unfinished masterpiece *Aesthetic Theory* where he polemically wrote: "Recommending jazz and rock-and-roll instead of Beethoven does not demolish the affirmative lie of culture but rather furnishes barbarism and the profit interest

---

17 Gandesha and Hartle, in Farina and Marino 2018, pp. 7-9.
18 GS 17, p. 77 (Adorno 2002b, p. 473).
19 GS 14, pp. 199-218 (Adorno 1976, pp. 21-38).
20 GS 10/1, pp. 337-345 (Adorno 1991b, pp. 97-106).
21 GS 17, pp. 10-11.

of the culture industry with a subterfuge. The allegedly vital and uncorrupted nature of such products is synthetically processed by precisely those powers that are supposedly the target of the Great Refusal. These products are the truly corrupt"[22].

Beside this, I also think that (2) from what I have called an *orthodox* Adornian point of view, a pseudo-artistic operation of this kind (where the concept of "pseudos", beside the concept of commodity itself, can be seen as the guiding-concept of Adorno's entire aesthetics of popular music[23]) should be understood as actually endangering the reputation of the critical theorist himself/herself and the legitimacy of his/her own thinking. From this point of view, writing a popular music song-hit on the critical thought and praxis of someone like Angela Davis (or, in my previous example used for my paper on System Of A Down, a song-hit on mass murder and genocide) makes the latter fall prey to the logic of the commodification of culture that the culture industry is based upon and actually fulfils, thus perverting the ideas and, in a sense, the reputation of the critical theorist.

We obviously don't have at our disposal explicit statements of Adorno on the specific case of rock songs dedicated to Angela Davis, since Adorno prematurely died in 1969, before the events of Davis's trial and arrest took place and hence also before the politically committed rock songs for her were written and sung. Apropos of their relationship, as we can learn from Adorno's biography Angela Davis took part to some of his teaching activities in the mid/late 1960s:

> In order to provide an adequate forum for a truly substantive discussion of *Negative Dialectics*, Adorno offered two regular philosophy seminars in the summer semester 1967 and the winter semester 1967-8 so as to create an opportunity for the book to be examined in detail. The high level of the seminar was guaranteed by the fact that it was attended not only by Horkheimer on occasion, but also by a whole series of assistants and colleagues of Adorno's from both philosophy and sociology. These included Werner Becker, Herbert Schnädelbach, Arend Kulenkampff and Karl-Heinz Haag. Among the students, of whom there were very many, despite the need

---

22 GS 7, pp. 473 (Adorno 2002a, pp. 319-320).
23 See Marino 2018.

to register officially, were Americans such as Angela Davis and Irving Wohlfahrt, as well as a number of people who were later to make their mark in university teaching as the younger representatives of critical theory.[24]

Also Davis' own autobiographical reflections testify the importance for her of studying with Adorno (beside, of course, the importance and influence of her teacher's lectures and writings: Marcuse). So, for example, she writes:

> During the summer after my studies in France, I had spent several weeks in Frankfurt attending a few of Adorno's lectures, and getting to know some of the students there. [...] Later I read all of Adorno's and Horkheimer's works that had been translated into English or French, in addition to Marcuse's writings. In this way I acquainted myself with their thought, which was collectively known as Critical Theory. [...] During that last year at Brandeis, I made up my mind to apply for a scholarship to study philosophy at the University of Frankfurt. Marcuse confirmed my conviction that this was the best place to study, given my interest in Kant, Hegel and Marx. [...] During the first weeks [scil. in Frankfurt], I didn't understand a word of what Adorno was saying. Not only were the concepts difficult to grasp, but he spoke his own special aphoristic variety of German. It was a consolation to discover that most German students attending his lectures for the first time were having almost as much trouble understanding Adorno as I. [...] Frankfurt was a very intensive learning experience. Stimulating lectures and seminars conducted by Theodor Adorno, Jürgen Habermas, Professor Haag, Alfred Schmidt, Oskar Negt. Tackling formidable works, such as all three of Kant's Critiques and the works of Hegel and Marx (in one seminar, we spent an entire semester analyzing about twenty pages of Hegel's *Logic*).[25]

Although – as I said – we unfortunately don't have at our disposal explicit statements of Adorno on the specific example that I am referring to in this contribution, we can fortunately hear from his own voice his thoughts about politically committed rock songs on other subjects of great interest for critical theorists in those

---

24 Müller-Doohm 2005, p. 440.
25 Davis 1988, pp. 135, 139, 142.

same years, like the Vietnam war. In fact, a short fragment of an interview with Adorno regarding a certain kind of *engagé* popular music typical of the late 1960s, now available on YouTube, is highly representative of his position (and extremely interesting for my purposes here), for example when he argues that *all* attempts

> to bring political protest together with "popular music" – that is, with entertainment music – are [...] *doomed from the start*. The *entire sphere* of popular music, even there where it dresses itself up in modernist guise, is to such a degree inseparable from the *Warencharakter*, from consumption, from the cross-eyed transfixion with amusement, that [all] attempts to outfit it with a new function remain *entirely* superficial. And I have to say [Adorno adds] that when somebody sets himself up, and for whatever reason [accompanies] maudlin music by singing something or other about Vietnam, [...] I find this song *unbearable* (*nicht zu ertragen*), in that by taking the Terrible or the Horrendous (*das Entsetzliche*) and making it something *consumable*, it ends up wringing something like consumption-qualities out of it.[26]

Adorno's idea is that a merely "consumable" (and, for this reason, "unbearable") work, like a popular music song-hit with its commodity character – due to its standardized musical *form* (which, in its dialectical relationship with the dimension of the artwork's *content*, represents one of the most important aspects of Adorno's entire philosophy of art[27]), and so due to its standardized musical material that eventually undergoes the process of manipulation by the culture industry known as "plugging"[28] –, eventually proves to be capable of turning *everything* it uses as subject or content into something "consumable": that is, capable of extorting something like consumption-qualities from *everything*, be it the Vietnam war, a mass murder or genocide, global hunger or even the critical thought of a radical theorist and feminist like Davis. So, for Adorno, writing one of those "unbearable" pop-rock songs

---

26   Interview with Adorno available at: www.youtube.com/watch?v=Xd7Fhaji8ow.
27   See GS 7, pp. 205-243, 431-438, 524-530 (Adorno 2002a, pp. 136-163, 290-295, 353-357).
28   Adorno 2006a, pp. 290-298.

that he disliked and considered as "commodities in the strict sense" on someone who aims to express a *protest* against the growing commodification of culture and life, logically implies making him/her run the risk of being commodified in turn, i.e. to be turned into a mere commodity. From this perspective, The Rolling Stones' song "Sweet Black Angel" on Angela Davis, or John Lennon's song "Angela", being "light popular music" and hence mere commodities "distributed on a mass-scale" and mere "consumer good[s]"[29], cannot help commodifying the latter's figure and thinking, and cannot help depriving it of what we may define its negative-critical potential and its truth content, thus turning it vice-versa into an affirmative-apologetic and hence "untrue" product[30].

From what I have defined so far an *orthodox* Adornian perspective, the result of writing songs on Auschwitz or the genocide of the Armenian is thus the commodification of these events (as explained in my previous work on this topic that I made reference to above); and the result of writing songs on a critical theorist is the commodification of critical theory: "Angela Davis as a commodity", as the title of this contribution reads. However, as I said, it is my firm conviction that a rigorous critical theorist like Adorno requires, for the very nature of his philosophy, a *critical* attention and a critical study, rather than an *acritical* and merely celebrative one, so that one must always try to philosophize dialectically "with Adorno" and at the same time "against Adorno". A basic and indeed essential characteristic of Adorno's theory, namely its radically dialectical nature (aimed to free dialectic from its historically deeply-rooted tendency "to achieve something positive by means of negation"; aimed to "free dialectics from such affirmative traits without reducing its determinacy"[31]), is of great help to this aim, so to speak. The need to be "dialectical, all too dialectical" in developing a theory of art that also includes new artistic forms connected to the transformations underwent by the artwork in the age of its industrial producibility and technological

---

29 Adorno 2006a, p. 278.
30 On this interpretation of the true/untrue dichotomy, or better dialectical relationship, in Adorno, I allow myself to remind the reader of my recent book *Le verità del non-vero* (Marino 2019, in particular pp. 21-76).
31 GS 6, p. 9 (Adorno 2004, p. XIX).

reproducibility, as a basic requirement for an aesthetic theory really up to this task and aimed to avoid the aging of aesthetics in contact with modern art[32], clearly emerges in all of Adorno's writings on this topic, also including the most important and philosophically substantial letters in his long correspondence with Benjamin during the 1930s[33].

A dialectically conceived (and even more a negative-dialectically conceived) philosophical aesthetics must in principle expect (because of its very nature, so to speak) the possibility of a dialectical development and indeed dialectical reversal. Like its analog at a purely theoretical level, i.e. negative dialectics, an aesthetics of this kind must accept to run the risk of appearing fragile and vertiginous, inasmuch as "the vertigo which this causes is an *index veri;* the shock of inconclusiveness, the negative as which it cannot help appearing in the frame-covered, neverchanging realm, is true for untruth only"[34]. So, *on the one hand,* Adorno's account of mass culture and the culture industry appears superior and more "dynamical" than other ones precisely because of its dialectical nature, strength and efficacy[35]. This becomes clear, in my opinion, when his dialectical approach is compared, for example, to Clement Greenberg's and Dwight MacDonald's more "static" and purely dualistic conceptions of the avant-garde/kitsch

---

32 See GS 7, pp. 493-505 (Adorno 2002a, pp. 332-340); GS 10/1, pp. 291-301, 432-453.
33 See, in particular, Adorno's letters to Benjamin from August 2, 1935, from March 18, 1936, and from November 10, 1938 (now in Adorno and Benjamin 1999). A careful and detailed analysis and interpretation of these letters in the context of the Adorno/Benjamin correspondence has been provided by Chitussi 2010, pp. 13-118.
34 GS 6, p. 43 (Adorno 2004, p. 32).
35 In some contributions Adorno explains that for him "culture industry" is a more fitting and precise definition in comparison to "mass culture" (see GS 10/1, p. 337 [Adorno 1991b, p. 98]). However, he also sometimes makes use of this quite common and usual term ("mass culture"), and the latter is used by Horkheimer in the title of his essay from 1941 (the same year of Adorno's seminal essay "On Popular Music") "Art and Mass Culture" (Horkheimer 2002, pp. 273-290). On Horkheimer's account of mass culture and its relationship with Adorno's own contributions on the same topic, see the essays collected in Emery 2018.

relation and the high culture/mass culture relation[36], or also to Guy Debord's somewhat rigid, inflexible and totalizing claims on *"everything* that was directly lived" that has now *completely* "receded into a representation", on "the world of the commodity dominating *all* living experience", on "the commodity [that] has succeeded in *totally* colonizing social life" and "society's *entire sold labour* [that] has become a *total* commodity"[37]. On the other hand, however, it must be also admitted that Adorno's "critique [of popular music]" is probably "less dialectical than is the case when he addresses art music"[38] (for example when he addresses dialectically the adventures and misadventures of Schönberg's expressionist atonality and then dodecaphony).

In my view, this becomes quite clear in Adorno's treatment of the serious/popular music distinction, which, although immediately freeing this distinction from the mere "complex vs. simple" criterion, is sometimes dualistically, dichotomously and so a little bit "undialectically" traced back by him to the sole criterion of standardization, that which may also attract on him to some extent the same criticism of "loss of dialectical consistency" and of "simplification which undermines [...] its fundamental truth"[39] that he had directed at Benjamin's conceptions of image, art and aura[40]. Indeed, Adorno's aesthetics of popular music is sometimes focused in a somewhat rigid way on the criterion of the latter's *totally* standardized character, although what he aimed to was to develop *at all levels* a philosophy "more dialectical than the dialectic"[41] (as he writes about the essay form). If we understand this, and if we adopt what I have previously defined

---

36 See Greenberg 1939 (reprinted 1957) and MacDonald 1960 (reprinted 2011). By the way, it can be interestingly observed that Adorno makes reference to Greenberg's theory of avant-garde vs. kitsch in his *Philosophy of New Music* (GS 12, p. 19 [Adorno 2006b, p. 13]), whereas many years later MacDonald explicitly quotes Adorno's essay "On Popular Music" in his famous work on masscult and midcult (MacDonald 2011, pp. 5, 27).
37 Debord 2005, §§ 1, 37 and 42, pp. 7, 17 and 21 (my emphasis).
38 Leppert 2002, p. 331.
39 Adorno and Benjamin 1999, pp. 105-106.
40 As Adorno critically writes to Benjamin in his letter from March 18, 1936: "What I should like to postulate, therefore, is *more* dialectics" (Adorno and Benjamin 1999, p. 131).
41 GS 11, p. 28 (Adorno 1991a, p. 19).

an *unorthodox* and critical approach towards Adorno's aesthetics of popular music (instead than a merely celebrative and acritical one), then it becomes possible, among other things, to also potentially argue in favor of *some* popular music song-hits that, notwithstanding their undeniable commodity character (being in any case products realized and commercialized by the culture industry) and notwithstanding their use of a musical material that is standardized in principle (because Adorno is right in claiming this, in my view), are nevertheless capable to develop non-standardized, i.e. original, often brilliant musical solutions with regard to both form and content.

As such, Adorno's aesthetics of popular music does not seem to open to even the possibility of a non-standardized use of standardized musical materials[42]. But this is something that, in my view, quite often occurs in the field of popular music, and it is something that, when applied to the musical treatment of certain politically committed topics (like genocide, in the case of the example of songs on genocide that I used in my previous works, or like the ideas of a critical theorist in the case of the example of Angela Davis that I am using here), can actually turn a popular music song-hit into a powerful vehicle to spread a certain message *without at the same time* reducing the song to something like a political pamphlet that only uses the music as a mere means to an end, which would be obviously inappropriate for a work of art where "the quintessence of all elements of logicality, or, more broadly, coherence [...], is form"[43]. Whereas, in turn, it is true that merely standardized and pseudo-individualized popular music song-hits that are perhaps praiseworthy on the level of *contents* expressed and hence from a purely ethical-political point of view, but are desperately lacking and insufficient on the level of *form* and hence from a strictly aesthetic point of view, actually run the risk of missing the point. That is, they run the risk of weakening the power of the critical message or content that they want to convey, rather than strengthening it (because, indeed, "an

---

42   I borrow this idea from Mecacci 2011, p. 98.
43   GS 7, p. 211 (Adorno 2002a, p. 140).

enormous quantity of popular music is precisely what Adorno claimed"[44]).

The question of *form* plays an important role in Adorno's explicit preference for serious music in comparison to popular music, not due to the former's complexity and the latter's simplicity, but rather to the former's (according to him) non-standardized formal character and the latter's *completely* standardized formal character. As he explains:

> The way in which one organizes this musical context in music is known as musical form. [...] [P]op songs also have a certain form. In fact, a form you are all accustomed to. If we now succeed in showing you the sense of this form with these very simple pop songs, that is to say, showing you what purpose is served by this form, and if we can fall back on your own experience with this form, that will greatly facilitate a different task: that of understanding the sense of musical form when dealing with less standardized products. And I hope that by doing this we will also achieve something else: that you come to understand, in a precise musical sense, the difference between light and serious music, and why we consider ourselves entitled to consider serious music something better than light music.[45]

However, even a quick look at the history of popular music in the last fifty or sixty years shows that there has been plenty of pop-rock and jazz music capable to escape the (for Adorno instead inescapable) "power of the banal [that] extends over the entire society", and thus capable to fulfill the "flight from the banal"[46] that he considered the task of music in the modern age, and sometimes also capable "to bring chaos into order" that he considered the task of all art today[47]. And even a quick look at the history of popular music in the last fifty or sixty years shows how the question concerning commitment (that, as has been noted before, Adorno often focused on in his aesthetic works) has played a relevant and sometimes absolutely decisive role in it. It may suffice here to remind the reader of such great meetings

---

44 Leppert 2002, p. 345.
45 Adorno 2006a, pp. 257-258.
46 GS 14, p. 19 (Adorno 1991b, p. 34).
47 GS 4, § 143, p. 253 (Adorno 2005, p. 222).

and events as the festival of Woodstock (1969), the "No Nukes" concerts (1979), the "Live Aid" and "Live 8" benefit concerts (1985, 2005), and the "Human Rights Concerts" in favor of Amnesty International (1986-88), or to remind the reader of the *engagé* pop-rock songs of such relevant artists as, for example, Joan Baez, Bob Dylan, John Lennon, Crosby, Stills, Nash & Young, Peter Gabriel, Bruce Springsteen, Sting, Simple Minds, U2, and still others. As explained in my previous work "Writing Songs after Auschwitz", the case of a *popular* heavy metal band like System of a Down (namely, a 40 million records-selling band that has proved to be able to spread information and raise a very broad audience awareness about what happened in Armenia and Turkey in 1915-16, and particularly about how those events have been recognized and understood, or vice-versa unrecognized and misunderstood, in the following decades), or the analogous case of a *popular* TV series like *Holocaust* (broadcasted in 1978 on NBC, aired one year later in West Germany and watched by about 20 million German viewers, bringing the matter of the genocide of the Jewish people to widespread public attention in an unprecedented way) and the attention and comments it raised (among which the philosophical observations of a relevant philosopher like Günther Anders), can be good examples for the defense of the *aesthetic legitimacy* of some forms of politically committed popular art that escape Adorno's criticism of total standardization and complete commodification and his consequential fear of the loss of both aesthetic and political efficacy (given the tight connection, and indeed the intertwinement of these dimensions, in Adorno's conception of the truth content of art).

In my view, the fundamental concept that requires to be rethought, in order to develop the kind of critical rethinking of an aesthetics of popular music "with Adorno/against Adorno" that I have in mind, is the concept of *musical material*, which I consider as *the* fundamental basis of Adorno's *entire* philosophy of music, as can be seen from its widespread and detailed use in his works on both serious music and popular music[48]. In fact, Adorno's conception is based on what has been emphatically

---

[48] See, for example, GS 12, pp. 38-42 (Adorno 2006b, pp. 31-34) and Adorno 2006a, pp. 280-290.

defined by some scholars as a veritable "philosophy of the history of music"[49] that, on the basis of precise ideas about the historical development of the musical material, conceives of Schönberg's music as the somehow secret *telos* of the history of modern music, with the Beethovenian paradigm of music as development (compared and opposed to the paradigm of music as repetition) as constant reference point[50]. It is also for this reason, I argue, that in his musicological writings after the Second World War Adorno seemed to have difficulty identifying a valid counterpart in the 1950s-1960s to what atonality and dodecaphony had been in the 1910s-1930s. The writings were therefore characterized, almost without exception, by the strong emphasis put on the difficulties in composing music in the new situation. In my view, such relevant and often convincing (but nonetheless highly problematic and often aporetic) essays from the 1950s and 1960s as "The Aging of the New Music", "The Prehistory of Serial Music", "The Function of Counterpoint in New Music", "Criteria of New Music", "Music and Technique", "Vers une musique informelle", "Form in the New Music" or finally "Difficulties" precisely testify this fact[51]. Albrecht Wellmer has emphasized the role played by all these factors in Adorno's philosophical musicology[52], expressing some critical comments on his

> Begriff des musikalischen Fortschritts, der diesen Fortschritt *allein* auf der Linie Beethoven-Brahms, Wagner-Schönberg (in seinen verschiedenen Phasen bis zur Zwölftontechnik) sieht, eine Linie, die dann schließlich zum Serialismus der Nachkriegsavantgarde führte. Zwar ist Adornos Kritik sowohl an der Zwölftontechnik wie später am Serialismus bekannt; aber er betrachtete letzlich beide "Phasen" der Musik, gemessen am geschichtlichen "Stand des Materials", doch

---

49 Zurletti 2000, p. 508.
50 This has been convincingly explained, among others, by Arbo 1991.
51 See, respectively, GS 14, pp. 143-167 (Adorno 2002b, pp. 181-202); GS 16, pp. 68-84 (Adorno 1999, pp. 54-68); GS 16, pp. 145-169 (Adorno 1999, pp. 123-144); GS 16, pp. 170-228 (Adorno 1999, pp. 145-196); GS 16, pp. 229-248 (Adorno 1999, pp. 197-214); GS 16, pp. 493-540 (Adorno 2002c, pp. 269-322); GS 16, pp. 607-627; GS 17, pp. 253-291 (Adorno 2002b, pp. 646-679).
52 The definition of "philosophical musicology" was first coined by the Italian musicologist Luigi Rognoni on the occasion of the Italian translation of Adorno's *Philosophy of New Musik* (see Rognoni 1966).

als *notwendige* Durchgangsstadien der musikalischen Entwicklung im Zuge der Überwindung der Tonalität und hin zu einer befreiten, nachtonalen Musik [...]. Gegen Adornos *unilinearen* Begriff des musikalischen Fortschritts und die damit verbundene Vorstellung eines mit Bezug auf mögliches authentisches Komponieren gleichsam *eindeutig bestimmten* Entwicklungsstandes des musikalischen Materials hat sich nicht erst im Zeitalter der Postmoderne Protest erhoben; er war vielmehr *von allem Anfang an* kontrovers [...]. Der *Pluralismus* musikalischer Verfahren [...] ist nicht der postmodernistische Pluralismus des *anything goes* [...]. Die Neue Musik selbst hat sich in mancher Hinsicht nach ihren Rändern hin geöffnet, sei es im Sinn einer Infragestellung der Unterscheidung zwischen "höherer" und "niederer" Kunst [...], sei es im Sinn einer *Öffnung* zum Pop- oder Improvisationsmusik hin, oder sei es schließlich im Sinn einer computergesteuerten Klanginstallationskunst.[53]

The fundamental problem probably lies in Adorno's – surely fascinating but also, in my view, somehow prejudiced – concept of the musical material and its dialectical movement. In fact, his philosophical interpretation of the history of modern music rests to a great extent on the basic presupposition of a precise tendency underlying the historical development of musical means from the tonal system to atonality and finally to twelve-tone music. Not by chance, at the beginning of the *Philosophy of New Music* (probably his musicological masterpiece) Adorno explicitly and emphatically asserts the "historical necessity" of the development of "the compositional material" that "contract[s] and expand[s] in the course of history" and that is characterized by precise, inescapable and infallible "laws of movement": "the process is inevitable"[54], as

---

[53] Wellmer 2005, pp. 256-261 (my emphasis). Wellmer goes so far as to speak of a "Fixierung auf die deutsch-österreichische Musiktradition" in Adorno's one-sided orientation "an der musikalischen Traditionslinie Beethoven-Brahms-Schönberg, [...] soweit es die 'syntaktische' Organisation der musikalischen Zeit betrifft, [und] an der Traditionslinie Beethoven-Wagner-Schönberg [...], soweit es die Tendenzen zur Auflösung der Tonalität betrifft" (p. 261), eventually drawing some interesting conclusions also on the culture industry and pop-rock and jazz music in the final part of his contribution (pp. 263-278).

[54] GS 12, pp. 38-39, 71 (Adorno 2006b, pp. 31, 57). On Adorno's conception of the development of the musical material in the contemporary age, applied

he writes apropos of the delicate equilibrium between freedom and unfreedom in the *neue Musik*. However, this conception sometimes gives the impression of being a sort of top-down schema: that is, a pre-planned framework imposed from above to actual musical phenomena that ultimately leads to exclude many other forms of music expression (in the very first instance *all* kinds of popular music) from those considered by Adorno as legitimate ones for the contemporary age, simply because they ignore the supposed inevitable character of dodecaphony and/or still make use of traditional musical means[55]. Traditional musical means and materials like, for example, major/minor chords, time signatures with regular or symmetrical beat patterns, a certain length and structure of the songs etc., that are precisely what the most part of contemporary popular music makes use of.

Referring once again to the examples mentioned before, it is true that songs like The Rolling Stones' "Sweet Black Angel" or John Lennon's "Angela" employ what we may call standardized musical materials, just like the Quartetto Cetra's "Angela" or the Canzoniere Internazionale's "Canzone per Angela Davis". However, while the latter clearly represent pure cases of entertainment based on the clichés, banalities, trivialities and standardized/commodified forms of popular music in its worst form (and thus fail from an aesthetic point of view, consequently falling prey to the identification/assimilation power of society and turning Angela Davis' critical thinking into an object of pure amusement), the former seem to exhibit at least to some extent the capacity to employ standardized musical materials in a non-standardized way or a genuinely individualized way (and not a merely pseudo-individualized way). From an Adornian point of view, this has relevant implications or consequences at *both* an aesthetic and

---

to all kinds of music (from atonality to dodecaphony to neoclassicism to jazz), see also his fascinating "Nineteen Contributions on the New Music" from 1942 that form a part of his "Theory of New Music" as a whole (GS 18, pp. 57-87).

55 "[W]e should be [...] wary of the idea that only one idiom is suitable for all musicians working at any given time", as observed by Theodore Gracyk in his essay "Adorno, Jazz, and the Reception of Popular Music" (in Gracyk 1996, p. 152).

a political level: in short, like "good serious music"[56] is somehow capable for him to resist the process of assimilation even under the (for him) quasi-totalitarian conditions of the culture industry in the age of the administered world, I suggest that also "good popular music" may prove capable to do this, namely to be the vehicle of real, genuine, authentic and powerful resistance, and not merely of pseudo-rebellion as Adorno seems to argue in the abovementioned fragment on the songs of protest against the Vietnam war.

At this point, of course, it might be objected that rock musicians like Frank Zappa, King Crimson, Genesis, Brian Eno, Pink Floyd, Sonic Youth or still others have experimented with musical materials that, in comparison to straight 4/4 rhythms or simple major/minor chords (even if embellished with melodic and harmonic solutions that partially suspend the standard function of chords in the tonal system), may appear as avant-gardist, original, "freaking-out" and "absolutely free" (freely adapting here Zappa's famous titles to my purposes). However, to such an objection I would reply or, as it were, counter-object: (1) that Zappa, Fripp or Eno represent the exception rather than the rule in contemporary popular music, and so it can be problematic to assume them as paradigmatic in this context; and (2) that *anyway* from an orthodox Adornian point of view even Pink Floyd's wildest and most dissonant experimentations in "Interstellar Overdrive", "Careful with That Axe, Eugene" or "A Saucerful of Secrets", for example, should be critically understood as pseudo-avant-garde attempts to replicate in the field of popular music what had already been successfully experimented in the field of truly avant-garde music and had meanwhile aged and got old: namely, a stage of development of the musical material that serious music had already got through and overcome, and hence "[a] shock which no longer shocks, and thus succumbing"[57]. It is true, indeed, that in a few late works, such as the chapter on popular music in his *Introduction to the Sociology of Music*, Adorno concedes that the so-called "evergreens" can sometimes be characterized by a genuine and indeed indescribable musical quality[58], but these admissions

---

56   Adorno 2006a, p. 284.
57   Marcuse 1972, p. 116.
58   GS 14, p. 215 (Adorno 1976, p. 35).

should not be overemphasized and should be understood as rare and above all circumstantial acknowledgments that only represent an exception and not the rule. As such, in my view they have no real impact on Adorno's fundamental conception of the standardized character of *all* popular music that apparently undergoes no changes or second thoughts from the early 1930s to the late 1960s.

If many experimental compositions and performances in rock music, especially in the late 1960s and 1970s, actually displayed melodic movements, harmonic structures or rhythmic patterns that were really surprising and sometimes shocking for pieces of light music, this does *not* imply that, from what I have called an *orthodox* Adornian perspective, this search for unheard solutions while remaining in the context of popular music may prove capable to finally emancipate the latter from being doomed to aesthetic failure and from being a mere decoration of empty time. Adorno never changed his general views on jazz improvisation (considered by him as the most drastic example of the specific feature of popular music called "pseudo-individualization"[59]) from his first essay "Farewell to Jazz" (1933) up to some critical remarks on jazz in his unfinished *Aesthetic Theory*[60], notwithstanding all the relevant changes occurred in jazz improvisation from Dixieland to swing to be-bop to free jazz. An exemplary proof of this fact can be found in the opening paragraph of Adorno's last essay specifically focused on jazz, "Perennial Fashion – Jazz" from 1953 (twenty years after his first essay on jazz[61]), and also in

---

59 Adorno 2006a, p. 288.
60 See GS 7, p. 177 (Adorno 2002a, p. 116), where he still talks of a veritable "antithesis of Beethoven and jazz".
61 "For almost fifty years, since 1914 when the contagious enthusiasm for it broke out in America, jazz has maintained its place as *a mass phenomenon*. Its method, all declarations of propagandistic historians notwithstanding, has remained *essentially unchanged* [...]. Jazz is music which fuses the most rudimentary melodic, harmonic, metric and formal structure with the ostensibly disruptive principle of syncopation, yet *without ever really disturbing* the crude unity of the basic rhythm, the identically sustained metre, the quarter-note. This is not to say that nothing has happened in jazz. [...] The wild antics of the first jazz bands from the South, New Orleans above all, and those from Chicago, have been toned down with the growth of commercialization and of the audience, and continued scholarly efforts to recover some of this original animation, whether called 'swing' or 'bebop', *inexorably succumb* to commercial requirements [...]. Yet *none*

a passage from his lesson on February 5, 1959 in the context of his lecture course on aesthetics from the winter semester 1958-59 (namely a legendary period for jazz, considering that 1959 is the year in which Miles Davis' *Kind of Blue*, John Coltrane's *Giant Steps* and Ornette Coleman's *The Shape of Jazz to Come* were recorded and/or published), where we explains to his students: "I think that phenomena such as jazz [...] are connected to the fact that people actually affirm and internalize their own reification in such phenomena, their own transformation into customers, and in a sense enjoy the fact that they themselves are also contained in the same mechanism – whereas they resist anything that is not already in it, anything that does not possess this particular immanence within the cultural scene"[62].

On this basis, I have reason to believe that he would have subsumed under the concept of "pseudo-individualization" also The Beatles' or Pink Floyd's or Frank Zappa's experimentations. In a very few passages of some of his late musicological or pedagogical works, for example, Adorno refers to The Beatles that had meanwhile become "more popular than Jesus" (in John Lennon's famous and quite provocative remark from March 1966). While Adorno denies that The Beatles, and thus rock 'n' roll in general, should be compared to barbarity as such (although their cult is for him a symptom of barbarism)[63], he also claims that the

---

of this alters the fact that jazz has in its essence remained static, nor does it explain the resulting enigma that millions of people seem never to tire of its *monotonous attraction*" (GS 10/1, p. 123 [Adorno 1997, p. 119: my emphasis]). Furthermore, after having been criticized by the German jazz musicologist Joachim-Ernst Berendt because of his enduring prejudices against jazz expressed in "Perennial Fashion – Jazz" notwithstanding the relevant changes occurred in jazz throughout the decades, Adorno did not soften his accusations but even sharpened them, eventually replying to Berendt's "Kritik" with a "Replik zu einer Kritik der *Zeitlosen Mode*" where we read: "In diesem Sinn [...] gibt es in der Tat am Jazz nichts zu verstehen. Die Differenz der Jazztypen, aus der Berendt eine Weltanschauung macht, ist eine der Façon, nicht der Struktur des musikalischen Verfahrens" (GS 10/2, p. 806). For a recent reconstruction and detailed interpretation of Adorno's approach to jazz, see Matteucci 2018.

62 Adorno 2017a, p. 311 (Adorno 2017b, p. 324).
63 "Meine Generation hat den Rückfall der Menschheit in die Barbarei erlebt, in buchstäblichem, unbeschreiblichem und wahrem Sinn. [...]. Mit Barbarei meine ich nicht die Beatles, obwohl ihr Kult dazu gehört"

students' critical replies to their teacher's untrue preachments on supposedly eternal values by invoking The Beatles' presumed newness are even false for their part[64]; and above all he claims that while a sociological research on the effect and impact on The Beatles on contemporary society might be indeed tempting for him[65], this does not exclude the latter being completely part of a musical life that prevents music from being really alive due to the predominant social processes of commodification and reification exemplified at a purely musical level by the persistence of the now aged tonal system[66]. As he writes in his "Anmerkungen zum deutschen Musikleben" from 1966:

> Das Musikleben befindet sich, trotz seiner Stabilisierung in den Konsumentengewohnheiten nach dem Zweiten Krieg, latent, den künstlerischen Möglichkeiten und schließlich dem Wahrheitsgehalt nach, *in einer Krise*. [...] *Musik ist verstrickt in die Problematik der gesamten bürgerlichen Gesellschaft. Sie ist vom Warencharakter ergriffen* und allem, was er involviert. Ich habe einmal simpel gesagt, das Musikleben sei kein Leben für die Musik: es ist, unmittelbar oder vermittelt, eines für den Profit. *Noch was es anders will, wird unweigerlich fast vom Wirtschaftsmechanismus ergriffen.* [...] Daß heute in der Musik das gesellschaftlich Rezipierte und das um seiner gesellschaftlichen Wahrheit willen Geforderte in unversöhnlichen Gegensatz getreten sind, zeigt *die gesamte Unterhaltungsmusik. In ihr triumphiert der Warencharakter, indem er aller autonomen, durchgeformten Gestaltung absagt* [...]. Die Warengesellschaft hat zu einem Grad sich ausgebreitet und ihr Netz gesponnen, der einer veränderten gesellschaftlichen Struktur gleichkommt. Das scheint im Musikleben sichtbar zu werden. [...] *Der Massengeschmack ist durchaus nicht dem Dirigismus entgegengesetzt.* Dieser drängt keineswegs den Massen, zumal den Millionen, die erst durchs

---

(GS 10/2, p. 672). A more positive account of the cult for The Beatles in the 1960s can be found in Horkheimer's aphorism "Das Phänomen der Beatles" (1991, p. 403).

64 "Lehrer und Schüler tun sich gegenseitig Unrecht an, wenn jener von Ewigkeitswerten schwafelt, die im allgemeinen keine sind, und die Schüler zur Antwort darauf zur schwachsinnigen Verehrung der Beatles sich entschließen" (GS 10/2, p. 666).

65 "[...] eine Untersuchung über die Wirkung der Beatles mich ungemein lockt" (GS 10/2, p. 813).

66 GS 17, p. 176.

Radio mit Musik zusammenstoßen, etwas auf. [...] *Krassestes Symptom dessen ist die fast unbeschränkte Herrschaft der Tonalität im Gebotenen, während die Entwicklung der musikalischen Produktivkräfte längst die Tonalität gesprengt hat.* [...] Der musikalisch Gebildete und der, welcher sich bloß dafür hält, neigen dazu, *Phänomene wie die Beatles,* welche, manipuliert oder nicht, die Massen ergreifen, dem Bildungsverfall zuzuschreiben. Anders jedoch als in der bildenden Kunst und in der Dichtung, scheinen in der Musik die bedeutendsten Werke, gleichgültig, welches Prestige sie genießen, nie voll rezipiert worden zu sein. Das weckt Skepsis gegen Anschauungen vom Verfall, die leicht in Kulturpessimismus elitären Schlages ausarten. *Nicht, daß er den gegenwärtigen Zustand kritisiert, ist solchem Pessimismus vorzuwerfen,* sondern die Verklärung der Vergangenheit.[67]

It is not possible here to develop a full-blown critical analysis of the concept of the *musical material* in order to set it free from what I consider Adorno's quasi-teleological interpretation of its laws of movement ineluctably leading to twelve-tone music, so I will limit myself to a single example taken from the musical dimension of harmony (implicitly assuming that analogous examples can be provided for all other dimensions of music: melody, form, instrumentation, arrangement, rhythm, meter[68]). If Adorno's historical-philosophical conception of the laws of development of the musical material is right, then introducing a diminished seventh chord in a pop-rock song (just like introducing a syncopated rhythm in a jazz tune, to mention one of his favorite examples) does not change anything as far as the latter's standardized and merely pseudo-individualized character (and thus its untruth) is concerned: in fact, "[w]hat is decisive in the truth and falsity of chords is not their isolated occurrence. It is measurable exclusively by the total level of technique. The diminished seventh chord [...] is correct and filled

---

67 GS 17, pp. 170-171, 174, 176-177 (my emphasis). I borrow all these references to The Beatles made by Adorno from Maurizi 2018 (p. 145 note), but I probably interpret them in a partially different way from him.
68 For a convincing analysis of rock and jazz music's non-standardized, democratized treatment of rhythm, and indeed their polymetric (and not merely polyrhythmic) structure, that also draws philosophical conclusions from this musicological analysis, see Gracyk 1996, pp. 130-147.

with expression at the beginning of Beethoven's Sonata opus 111", but after the aging of tonality, understood as an entire reference system of sounds in all the dimensions of music[69], "the defunct diminished seventh chord [...] represents a state of technique that as a whole contradicts that of today"[70]. In order to rescue the very possibility to still make use of these and other similar musical means (widely employed especially in contemporary popular music[71]) without for this reason being automatically condemned to falsity and to the complete loss of any truth content, it is thus necessary to especially rethink Adorno's conception of the musical material's quasi-teleological development from tonality to atonality to dodecaphony up to his late and surely fascinating but also somehow vague ideal of a *musique informelle*.

Of course, it must be emphasized that the problem, for Adorno, is not that classical music is "serious" while popular music is "light" (although reconciling them has proved impossible for him since the time of Mozart's *Magic Flute*[72]), and not even that serious music is complex while popular music is simple, but rather that the former (or at least "good serious music", because there is also "bad serious music"[73]) is non-standardized while the latter is *always and necessarily* standardized. The problem, for me, is

---

69 I borrow the concept of "reference system of sounds" from Azzaroni 1997, pp. 209-283.
70 GS 12, pp. 40-41 (Adorno 2006b, p. 33).
71 As noted by Philip Tagg, however, the tonality of the music of our everydayness, or "everyday tonality", is probably different from the tonality of classical music, i.e. it makes use of different melodic and harmonic solutions, and anyway even the same harmonic structures employed in a different musical context acquire a different meaning (see Tagg 2011, pp. 17-33, 80-285).
72 "Until the end of prehistory, the musical balance between partial stimulus and totality, between expression and synthesis, between the surface and the underlying, remains as unstable as the moments of balance between supply and demand in the capitalist economy. *The Magic Flute*, in which the utopia of the Enlightenment and the pleasure of a light opera comic song precisely coincide, is a moment by itself. After *The Magic Flute* it was never again possible to force serious and light music together" (GS 14, p. 17 [Adorno 1991b, p. 32]).
73 Sibelius is probably Adorno's favorite example and thus his favorite polemical target in this field. As he writes, "anyone who lauds Sibelius' craftsmanship shows that he either does not know what musical craftsmanship is or that he does not know Sibelius" (Adorno 2006a, p. 208).

that *not all* popular music can be subsumed in such a strict and rigid way under the concept of standardization, i.e. *not all* popular music is completely standardized and pseudo-individualized; and this, in turn, does *not necessarily* depend on the technical level of the composers or performers of a certain pop-rock song or a certain pop-rock album (but the very same thing, of course, also holds true for jazz). This is made clear, for example, by the fact that many relatively simple compositions by songwriters like Bob Dylan, Leonard Cohen, Paul Simon, Neil Young or Lou Reed, or many very simple songs in the field of punk and hardcore music, are definitely less standardized and more original, sharp and aesthetically convincing than may relatively complex rock-suites or rock-symphonies by Yes or Emerson, Lake & Palmer or still other "progressive rock" bands, let alone some very sophisticated and at the same time very standardized and kitsch compositions by "progressive metal" or "symphonic metal" bands[74]. If so, then what is required to really do justice to such great musical experiences of the twentieth and also twenty-first century that fully belong to the realm of popular music but are nonetheless provided with a prominent truth content, and that may surely include Zappa, Fripp or Eno but also less sophisticated and "simpler" musicians like Dylan, Lennon or Cohen, is a broader and more general rethinking of the concept itself of the musical material and its development that sets it free from any idea of intrinsic, immanent and quasi-teleological laws of movement. Only this, in my view, can lead to what has been emphatically defined "a non-Schönberghian musical universe, devoid of and free from ineluctable gravitational pulls"[75] (as dodecaphony surely was for Adorno[76]).

---

74 On this topic, see Jacobsson 2013.
75 Salvatore 2000, p. 12.
76 "Twelve-tone music's urgency intensifies [...] once the schema of tonality – which legitimated the preponderance of individual tones – is canceled. Whoever has dealt closely with free atonality knows the distracting power of a melodic or bass tone that occurs for a second time before all the other tones have preceded it" (GS 12, p. 65 [Adorno 2006b, p. 52]). In writing "Whoever has dealt closely with free atonality" Adorno is probably referring also to his own early experiences as pupil of Alban Berg and composer of free atonal music. For an overview on Adorno's early "commuting between philosophy and music", see Müller-Doohm 2005, pp. 67-165.

A critical rethinking of Adorno's fundamental conception of the *musical material*, in turn, has profound implications and consequences also on his conception of the *commodity character* of popular music, as emerges from all his writings on these topics, from the final paragraphs of "On the Social Situation of Music" (1932) to "Farewell to Jazz" (1933), "On Jazz" (1936), "On the Fetish-Character in Music and the Regression of Listening" (1938) and "On Popular Music" (1941), up to parts of *Philosophy of New Music* (1949), "Perennial Fashion – Jazz" (1953), parts of *Introduction to the Sociology of Music* (1962), "Culture Industry Reconsidered" (1963) and even parts of *Aesthetic Theory* (1969). That is, rethinking the concept of *standardization* – that is at least in part derived from Adorno's philosophical interpretation scheme of the history of music and his idea of a rigorous development of the musical material in history – also leads to rethinking the concept of *commodification* that is closely connected to it[77]. Of course, this does *not* mean exchanging and confusing Adorno's concept of standardization with his concept of commercialization (that, as has been correctly noted, must be understood autonomously, differentiated from each other, and hence not confused[78]) but simply understanding the *relationship* between these two aspects, inasmuch as the commercial commodity character of popular music does not depend only on an "outer" dimension (as in the case of the manipulation that, for Adorno, all popular music undergoes under the name of "plugging"[79]) but also on an intrinsically musical dimension, namely on the inner constitution of a music that, for him, is *standardized* through and through, and for this reason is "a priori" *commodified* through and through.

So, asking once again the leading questions of the present contribution ("What happens when a critical theorist, namely someone who is supposed to develop a critical theory and praxis that protests against the growing commodification of culture and life in the contemporary age, becomes him- or herself a commodity? What happens when a critical theorist like Angela Davis becomes

---

[77] As Adorno writes, "increasing standardization [...] is bound up with the commodity character of music" (Adorno 2006a, p. 137).
[78] See Maurizi 2018 (p. 67 note), who correctly criticized Richard Middleton (1990) on this point.
[79] Adorno 2006a, p. 291.

the object of a commodity in the strict sense like The Rolling Stones' or John Lennon's song-hits?"), the answer must be now: "It depends". And yet, from an *orthodox* Adornian perspective, there seems to be no possible "It depends" answer, since for him not only "*all* 'light' and pleasant art has become illusory and mendacious today", "entertainment [...] today spreads over *the whole* of musical life", *all* "contemporary mass music [...] is *only* play as a repetition of prescribed models", and "*all* attempts to reform mass music and regressive listening on the basis of what exists [...] are fruitless"[80], but also, more in general, "*all* mass culture" (be it music, film, TV, comic strips, sport, fashion etc.) "is identical"[81].

According to Adorno, "the goods" produced by the culture industry are *all* characterized by an "identical character"[82], and the latter infects "*everything* with *sameness*": "*all* mass culture [...] is identical", it is "*nothing but business*", a sort of "trash [...] intentionally produce[d]" by the culture industry on the basis of a perverse "cycle of manipulation and retroactive need" aimed at suppressing "*any trace* of spontaneity"[83] in our aesthetic experience. Adorno goes as far as defining the culture industry as the "adversary [of] avant-garde art", inasmuch as the latter "serve[s] truth", unlike cinema, radio, popular music or magazines that merely represent for him "the aesthetic equivalent of power"[84] (although after the misadventures of dodecaphony and serial music in the 1950s/1960s he was perplexed about the avant-garde's capacity to preserve the truth content of art). For him, the "split between them", namely the split between serious, autonomous art and light, heteronomous art (which is mere entertainment or amusement, and indeed a false and untrue one because it fakes "lightness" and freedom while actually being for Adorno a mere ideological instrument of power and domination to occupy people's free time and make it unfree: an entertainment that does not really entertain but rather enslaves), expresses "the negativity of the culture which is the sum of both spheres": for Adorno, the "antithesis can be reconciled least of all by absorbing light art

---

80   GS 14, pp. 19, 30, 46-47 (Adorno 1991b, pp. 33, 43, 57-58 [my emphasis]).
81   GS 3, pp. 141-142 (Adorno and Horkheimer 2002, pp. 94-95 [my emphasis]).
82   GS 14, p. 27 (Adorno 1991b, p. 40).
83   GS 3, pp. 142-143 (Adorno and Horkheimer 2002, pp. 94-96 [my emphasis]).
84   GS 3, pp. 149, 151 (Adorno and Horkheimer 2002, pp. 101, 103).

into serious or vice-versa", which is however "what the culture industry attempts"[85]. The ideological value of the works produced by the culture industry also lies in their tendency to inspire in the consumers – at times dramatically defined by Adorno as "victims"[86] – an attitude of passive acceptance of the real in all its meaninglessness (while presenting it as meaningful, or even as the best world possible in the happy ending of Hollywood movies): "ideology becomes the emphatic and systematic proclamation of what is", "it exploits the cult of fact" in order to consolidate "the immutability of the existing circumstances" which thus take on "the aspect of fate"[87].

However, in doing so, Adorno's theory proves to be unable to differentiate what actually requires differentiation, because of its different nature: writing a popular music song-hit on Angela Davis (especially if the authors are songwriters like Bob Dylan, John Lennon or Mick Jagger and Keith Richards) is not the same as creating a t-shirt or a puppet of Walter Benjamin, for example. And still referring to the abovementioned examples, John Lennon's or The Rolling Stones' songs for Davis, in turn, on the basis of their intrinsic musical structure and the way they employ standardized musical materials in non-standardized ways, are not comparable to the Quartetto Cetra's song for Davis, unless we accept to completely lose sight of their incomparably different musical value (notwithstanding the similar musical material that they start from but that they elaborate then in very different ways). However, for Adorno "in *all* its branches [*scil.* the culture industry's branches], products which are tailored for consumption by masses [...] are manufactured [...] according to a plan", and thus *in the same way*: "cultural entities typical of the culture industry are no longer also commodities, they are commodities through and through"[88], and this applies for him to *all* the culture industry's products. As has been noted, from an Adornian perspective "the musics developed by the culture industries are *all* commodified

---

85 GS 3, p. 157 (Adorno and Horkheimer 2002, pp. 107-108).
86 GS 14, p. 36 (Adorno 1991b, p. 48). In his *Philosophy of New Music* Adorno explicitly speaks of "the violence that mass music inflicts on men", for example (GS 12, p. 69 [Adorno 2006b, p. 55]).
87 GS 3, pp. 170-171, 174 (Adorno and Horkheimer 2002, pp. 118-119, 122).
88 GS 10/1, pp. 337-338 (Adorno 1991b, pp. 98, 100).

musics and their appeal to the subject works *in the same way* as that of *all* commodities"[89]: "in radio, the film, industry, the variety act, cartoons – *everywhere* – Adorno saw the culture industry as the enemy of humanity and true feeling"[90].

This, however, makes his concept of the *commodification* of culture, just like his concept of *musical material* that I have referred to before, less dialectical and more rigid or, as it were, "monolithic" than one would expect from the twentieth-century dialectical philosopher *par excellence* (although, alternatively, one might also raise the suspect that such a rigid or "monolithic" concept is precisely what is expected by commodified dialectics, as opposed to a living person with idiosyncrasies). Being able to distinguish between different products of the culture industry, and thus developing a more nuanced conception of the cultural commodities that, in our widely aestheticized age, actually "create" the environment that we live in and confer a certain atmosphere or mood to our everydayness, is an important task for an aesthetics of popular art. A major problem in this field has often been represented precisely by the evident commodity character of the products of the so-called "industrial fine arts"[91]. In fact, the idea itself of an aesthetics of popular art aimed at showing that the latter deserves serious aesthetic attention has sometimes been challenged by the standard objection (also based on the persistence of certain aprioristic ideas on disinterest as the unique feature of real aesthetic pleasure, etc.) that these cultural products, inasmuch as they belong to the realm of commodities and are thus "corrupted" by undisinterested components, for this very reason (so reads the aprioristic objection) cannot be considered as works having a real significance, or, in Adorno's words, as works having a real truth content. On the basis of what has been said before, however, I argue that it is possible to share some of Adorno's basic premises and presuppositions, namely to accept the idea of the commodity character of the culture industry's products but to reverse some of his conclusions, or, as it were, to partially turn

---

[89] Witkin 2000, p. 155.
[90] Witkin 1998, p. 173. See also Witkin 2003, pp. 98-134.
[91] Vitta 2012, pp. 38-74, 125-192.

them upside down (also recognizing that he, no doubt like anyone else, had his own idiosyncrasies, just like I have mine).

In my view, it is possible indeed to argue in favor of the idea of a sometimes relevant aesthetic potential and truth content that may be present in much popular music (although not all, of course) notwithstanding its fundamental and undeniable commodity character. I would like to call this idea the "self-transcending commodities thesis", and by recurring to a kind of "by analogy argumentation" I argue that, *just like* individuals are surely conditioned by the society that they belong to, but not fully determined by it, and can therefore "transcend" at least to some extent its conditioning power; and *just like*, according to Adorno, an artwork is always a *res* but provided with an addendum ("the more"[92]) that allows it to "transcend" its basic reified character and to become a "self-transcending" *res* (a thing that is "more" than just a thing, as it were[93]); *so*, also works of the popular arts are surely conditioned by the context that they belong to, and hence by the culture industry as an organ of the administered world, but are nevertheless *not fully* determined by it, and are therefore capable to "transcend" it. Namely, they are capable to develop a partially autonomous character that, of course, may only last a season, as in the case of the fads that Adorno liked to compare to jazz styles, but that, especially in case of politically committed works on particular subjects, may also lead to significant aesthetic and *at the same time* political results which we may call their truth content and connect to the question of engagement. In a sense, aesthetically successful popular music song-hits are works that, performing a sort of aesthetic acrobatic turn, succeed in doing what Adorno himself self-consciously and paradoxically prescribed to philosophy and art in the age of their potential "liquidation", namely to be able to repeat the Baron Munchausen's gesture of "pulling himself out of the bog by his pig-tail": "nothing less is asked of the thinker today than that he should be at every moment both within things and outside them"[94]. In a similar way, nothing less is asked of the pop-rock musician today than that he/she should be "in the marketplace

---

92   GS 7, pp. 122-131 (Adorno 2002a, pp. 78-84).
93   GS 7, pp. 260-262 (Adorno 2002a, pp. 174-175).
94   GS 4, § 46, p. 83 (Adorno 2005, p. 74).

but not governed by the values of the marketplace"[95], struggling to compose and perform non-standardized music that nevertheless starts from standardized musical materials, more or less like negative dialectics' "cognitive utopia [...] to use concepts to unseal the non-conceptual with concepts, without making it their equal"[96].

Of course, this argumentation rests on a basic presupposition, namely on the idea that total control or complete domination cannot be achieved in the domain of the culture industry, just like, once again reasoning "by analogy", for a philosopher like Gadamer complete forgetfulness of Being cannot be achieved (in contrast to some theories of his teacher Heidegger)[97]. As has been noted, "Adorno underestimated the potential of [popular music] to emerge from the grip of the culture industry and to develop, as a cultural process, its own forms of resistance" (and underestimated the potentialities still present in the traditional musical materials that most popular music makes use of), and such a critical perspective "argues for a more subtle, less monolithic view of the dynamics of cultural processes such as [popular music] and their relationship to the culture industry": "it raises the question of the boundaries of the culture industry"[98]. Certain analyses and critical investigations of popular music and popular culture focused on so-called subcultural and oppositional styles have offered convincing insights and suggestions on these aspects, I think[99].

Raising the questions of the boundaries of the culture industry logically implies recognizing that the latter's conditioning power is mighty and sometimes overwhelming but limited, *not* unlimited, and *not* equally distributed in the same way in *all* products of the culture industry, let alone in *all* politically committed rock songs that may differ so much from each other not only because of their contents in the lyrics but also because of their musical form.

---

95 Robert Fripp's liner notes to his record *God Save the Queen* (quoted in Tamm 1990, p. 92).
96 GS 6, p. 21 (Adorno 2004, p. 10).
97 "Complete forgetfulness of being cannot be achieved", Gadamer claims in an interview, thus confirming that he does not follow Heidegger "when he says that only a God can save us" or when he talks about new gods and similar things (Gadamer 1988, p. 26).
98 Witkin 1998, p. 177.
99 See, for instance, Hebdgige 1979; Chambers 1986; Wilson 2003.

Focusing on the "standardized/non-standardized" character of a certain piece of music through an analysis of its musical material and the way it is employed can be a good criterion (much more useful and fitting than, say, the purely mechanical "simple/complex" or "lowbrow/highbrow" distinctions) to differentiate music provided or not provided with a broadly speaking "truth content", and we owe this criterion to Adorno's unique and penetrating analyses of popular music. Already in his pioneering contribution from 1932 "On the Social Situation of Music" he suggests replacing the usual "distinction between light and serious music" with "a different distinction" based on "the perspective of alienation" that differentiates between music that "unconditionally recognizes its commodity character and, refusing any dialectical intervention, orients itself according to the demands of the market", i.e. music "passive and undialectic [that] takes its place on the side of society", and music that "in principle does not accept the demands of the market" and "takes its place [...] on the side of music"[100]. However, the history of contemporary popular music testifies that, contra Adorno, this kind of differentiation between *true* (i.e. critical) and *untrue* (i.e. uncritical and passive) music can also be applied to pop-rock songs and can be of decisive importance in the case of politically committed songs in order to distinguish songs *meritoriously* committed to important causes that *miserably* drift into mediocrity and cliché territory in the end (many examples of very famous but also very kitsch pop songs could be mentioned here and assumed as representative of this trend) from songs dealing with certain politically committed topics that, due to their level of formal and stylistic elaboration, eventually escape *standardization* and thus free themselves from the clutches of *commodification*.

From this point of view, Adorno's method, capable to proceed from both the inside and the outside of the artwork and to deduce the social implications and hence also the truth content of music "from an analysis of the musical material itself"[101], still deserves great attention and to some extent remains unsurpassed as to its unique capacity to investigate the *aesthetic* dimension and the *socio-political* dimension in their dialectical intertwinement

---

100   GS 18, p. 733 (Adorno 20002b, p. 395).
101   Adorno 2006a, p. 279.

and their close relationship[102]. However, what is required is sometimes "a more fine-grained and concrete analysis of the various arts and the differing forms of their appropriation" which also includes, among other things, the capacity to differentiate between different kinds of music making use of different kinds of musical material and consequentially requiring more *intellectual* forms of appreciation (like the kind of "structural listening" theorized and recommended by Adorno[103]) or, instead, "more *somatic* forms of effort, resistance, and satisfaction" that may be the genuine expression of "a radically revised aesthetic with a joyous return of the somatic dimension which philosophy has long repressed"[104], and that for this reason need not necessarily be included in "contemporary habits of listening to light popular music" scornfully defined as "atomistic listening" or "commodity listening" gravitating only "about recognition" and not about genuine "music understanding"[105].

If "freedom is a constant struggle", as precisely Angela Davis invites us to think[106], then *aesthetically* successful examples of *politically* committed rock songs can help us in our struggle, can support us and encourage us not to let go of the courage and hope that are required "to embark on project[s]" aimed "to reach a just society", although always being lucidly aware that "the subcultures that originated" a certain protest or rebellion can be normalized, can "[go] mainstream" and be turned into "commodity consumption"[107], but also being aware that precisely courage and hope represent the conditions of possibility for action and perhaps also for truth[108]. It might be said that the final aim for a critical theorist is to gradually become aware of the real nature of what is, i.e. to increase one's critical consciousness of "the essence of the existing order" in order to penetrate and thus dissolve the "social

---

102 This has been correctly noted and also emphatically emphasized, among others, by Guanti 1999, pp. 486-487.
103 On structural listening applied to the understanding of new music (*neue Musik*), see for instance GS 15, pp. 188-248.
104 Shusterman 2000, p. 184.
105 Adorno 2006a, pp. 299-326.
106 See Davis 2015.
107 Arruzza, Bhattacharya and Fraser 2019, pp. 5, 35.
108 As Adorno writes, "hope, wrested from reality by negating it, is the only form in which truth appears" (GS 4, § 61, p. 110 [Adorno 2005, p. 98]).

context which induces blindness", eventually developing a kind of "enlightenment [that] is more than enlightenment" and that prepares for "a true praxis capable of overturning the status quo"[109]. If this is the final aim, then it should be acknowledged that certain kinds of popular music can serve to this goal and can legitimately support the thought and action of critical theorists, like Angela Davis in the example chosen here. As has been observed precisely about Davis and the role of popular culture and popular music in connection to emancipation processes and political action,

> for Davis, her former professor [*scil.* Marcuse] was an intellectually liberating figure [and] perhaps the most surprising aspect of his influence on Davis was how it shaped her vision of the utopian possibilities contained in art, literature and music. [...] Surely he had no sense of popular music as being resistant to the status quo, but rather regarded it as Adorno regarded jazz, part of the culture industry that kept the status quo in place. "He started to change. He had this very classical, European formation, so culture for him was high culture, but I think he later began to recognise that we shouldn't be concerned with high versus low culture. We should be concerned with the work that culture does". In her 1998 book *Blues Legacies and Black Feminism*, Davis wrote about how singers such as Gertrude "Ma" Rainey, Bessie Smith, and Billie Holiday "provided a cultural space for community-building among working-class black women [...] in which the coercions of bourgeois notions of sexual purity and 'true womanhood' were absent". Marcusean notions of art as a semi-autonomous zone or another dimension where utopias could be imagined in opposition to the dominant cultures it indicted infuse this book. Marcuse, following Adorno, who in turn was following Stendhal, wrote of art as offering *promesse du bonheur* [and] found that *promesse du bonheur* in 17th century Dutch painting, Goethe's *Wilhelm Meister*, the English novel of the 19th century and Thomas Mann; Angela Davis heard it in Bessie Smith and Billie Holiday.[110]

We, for our part, can perhaps hear the *promesse du bonheur* in John Lennon's or The Rolling Stones' songs of freedom in support of Angela Davis, or in "the lyrics and music of Bob Dylan" in which "the political dimension remains committed to the other, the

---

109 GS 3, pp. 44, 57, 59 (Adorno and Horkheimer 2002, pp. 20, 31, 33).
110 Jeffries 2017.

aesthetic dimension, which, in turn, assumes political value"[111], or in The Clash's vehemently political songs of protest, or in Ramones' "music as an amalgam of contradictions: *dialectic at a standstill*"[112], or in Fugazi's "three-minute access" negative aesthetics[113], or in System Of A Down's abovementioned political songs on the Armenian genocide, or in Pearl Jam's "riot act" songs against President Bush's infamous "patriot act", or in Eddie Vedder's sober but incisive refusal to be subjugated by a society that is "a crazy breed" and is grounded on "a greed with which we have agreed" (and with which, vice-versa, we should "disagree"), or finally in Rage Against The Machine's very emphatic invitations to consider "anger [as] a gift", to "fight the war [and] fuck the norm", and to oppose to the society's coercion to normalization and assimilation an explicit, all too explicit expression of the Great Refusal ("Fuck you, I won't do what you tell me"), also reminding us of the real nature of the enemy: "Yes, I know my enemies / They're the teachers who taught me to fight me / Compromise, conformity, assimilation, submission / Ignorance, hypocrisy, brutality, the elite / All of which are American dreams" – or, in a more Adornian fashion, all of which have always been Western civilization's dreams ever since its inception with "myth [that] is already enlightenment, and enlightenment [that] reverts to mythology"[114].

Bibliography

Adorno Th. W.
1970 ff. *Gesammelte Schriften* (quoted as GS), ed. by R. Tiedemann, Suhrkamp, Frankfurt a.M.
1976. *Introduction to the Sociology of Music*, trans. by E.B. Ashton, The Seabury Press, New York.
1991a. *Notes to Literature 1*, trans. by Sh. Weber Nicholsen, Columbia University Press, New York.
1991b. *The Culture Industry: Selected Essays on Mass Culture*, ed. by J.M. Bernstein, Routledge, London.

---

[111] Marcuse 1972, p. 117.
[112] Maurizi 2018, p. 184.
[113] See Campbell 2007.
[114] GS 3, p. 16 (Horkheimer and Adorno 2002, p. XVIII).

1992. *Notes to Literature 2*, trans. by Sh. Weber Nicholsen, Columbia University Press, New York.
1997. *Prisms*, trans. by S. and Sh. Weber, The MIT Press, Cambridge (MA).
1999. *Sound Figures*, trans. by R. Livingstone, Stanford University Press, Stanford (CA).
2002a. *Aesthetic Theory*, trans. by R. Hullot-Kentor, Continuum, London-New York.
2002b. *Essays on Music*, trans. by S.H. Gillespie et al., ed. by R.D. Leppert, The University of California Press, Berkeley.
2002c. *Quasi una Fantasia: Essays on Modern Music*, trans. by R. Livingstone, Verso, London-New York.
2004. *Negative Dialectics*, trans. by E.B.Ashton, Routledge, London-New York.
2005. *Minima Moralia: Reflections on a Damaged Life*, trans. by E. Jephcott, Verso, London-New York.
2006a. *Current of Music: Elements of a Radio Theory*, ed. by R. Hullot-Kentor, Polity Press, Cambridge-Malden (MA).
2006b. *Philosophy of New Music*, trans. and ed. by R. Hullot-Kentor, University of Minnesota Press, Minneapolis-London.
2017a. *Ästhetik (1958/59)*, ed. by E. Ortland, in *Nachgelassene Schriften*, vol. IV/3, Suhrkamp, Frankfurt a.M.
2017. *Aesthetics*, trans. by W. Hoban, Polity Press, Cambridge-Medford (MA).

Adorno Th. W. and Benjamin W.
1999. *The Complete Correspondence: 1928-1940*, trans. by N. Walker, Harvard University Press, Cambridge (MA).

Adorno Th. W. and Horkheimer M.
2002. *Dialectic of Enlightenment: Philosophical Fragments*, trans. by E. Jephcott, Stanford University Press, Stanford (CA).

Arbo A.
1991. *Dialettica della musica. Saggio su Adorno*, Guerini e Associati, Milano.

Arruzza C., Bhattacharya T. and Fraser N.
2019. *Feminism for the 99%: A Manifesto*, Verso, London-New York.

Azzaroni L.
1997. *Canone infinito. Lineamenti di teoria della musica*, Bologna, CLUEB.

Campbell C. J.
2007. "Three-Minute Access: Fugazi's Negative Aesthetic", in D. Burke et al. (ed.), *Adorno and the Need in Thinking: New Critical Essays*, University of Toronto Press, Toronto-Buffalo-London, pp. 278-295.

Chambers I.
1986. *Urban Rhythms: Pop Music and Popular Culture*, St. Martin's Press, New York.

Chitussi B.
2010. *Immagine e mito. Un carteggio tra Benjamin e Adorno*, Mimesis, Milano-Udine.

Church Gibson P.
2012. "Nuove alleanze: mondo dell'arte, case di moda e celebrità", in M. Pedroni and P. Volonté (ed.), *Moda e arte*, Franco Angeli, Milano, pp. 203-2018.

Davis A.
1988. *An Autobiography*, Random House, New York.
2015. *Freedom is a Constant Struggle*, Haymarket Books, Chicago (Ill.).

Debord G.
2005. *Society of Spectacle*, trans. by K. Knabb Rebel Press, London.

Emery N. (ed.)
2018. *Arte nuova e cultura di massa*, Mimesis, Milano-Udine.

Farina M. and Marino S. (ed.)
2018. "Forum on *Aesthetic Marx*, ed. by S. Gandesha and J. Hartle", in "Lebenswelt. Aesthetics and philosophy of experience", n. 13, pp. 1-23.

Gadamer H.-G.
1988. "Interview with Hans-Georg Gadamer", in "Theory, Culture, & Society", vol. 5, n. 1, pp. 25-34.

Gracyk Th.
1996. *Rhythm and Noise: An Aesthetics of Rock*, Duke University Press, Durham (NC).

Greenberg C.
1957. "Avant-Garde and Kitsch" (1939), in B. Rosenberg and D. Manning White (ed.), *Mass Culture: The Popular Arts in America*, The Free Press of Glencoe, New York, pp. 98-110.

Guanti G.
1999. *Estetica musicale. La storia e le fonti*, La Nuova Italia, Firenze.

Hebdige D.
1979. *Subculture: The Meaning of Style*, Routledge, London.

Iannilli G.L.
2018. "Entry: Aestheticization", in *International Lexicon of Aesthetics*, ed. by the SIE. Società Italiana di Estetica (available at: https://lexicon.mimesisjournals.com/international_lexicon_of_aesthetics_item_detail.php?item_id=14; last accessed: August 18, 2019)

Horkheimer M.
2002. "Art and Mass Culture", in *Critical Theory: Selected Essays*, trans. by M.J. O'Connell et al., Continuum, New York, pp. 273-290.

Jacobsson M.
2013. "*The Dance of Eternity*. Breve 'improvvisazione' su musica assoluta e *progressive metal*", in D. Ferdori and S. Marino (ed.), *Filosofia e popular music*, Mimesis, Milano-Udine, pp. 149-184.

Jeffries S.
2017. "The Effect of the Whip: The Frankfurt School and the Oppression of Women" (available at: https://www.versobooks.com/blogs/2846-the-effect-of-the-whip-the-frankfurt-school-and-the-oppression-of-women; last accessed: July 5, 2019).

Leppert R.
2002. "Introduction" and "Commentary" to Th. W. Adorno, *Essays on Music*, trans. by S.H. Gillespie et al., ed. by R.D. Leppert, The University of California Press, Berkeley.

MacDonald D.
2011. "Masscult and Midcult" (1960), in *Masscult and Midcult: Essays Against the American Grain*, New York Review of Books, New York.

Marcuse H.
1972. *Counterrevolution and Revolt*, Beacon Press, Boston.

Marino S.
2014. *La filosofia di Frank Zappa. Un'interpretazione adorniana*, Mimesis, Milano-Udine.

2017a. "Writing Songs After Auschwitz: Rethinking Adorno's Concept of Commitment and Aesthetics of Popular Music", in "Zeitschrift für Ästhetik und Allgemeine Kunstwissenschaft", vol. 62, n. 1, pp. 25-40.
2017b. "Auschwitz e *popular culture*: considerazioni estetico-politiche sulla presenza del genocidio nella cultura di massa", in M. Latini and E.S. Storace (ed.), *Auschwitz dopo Auschwitz. Poetica e politica di fronte alla Shoah*, Meltemi, Roma, pp. 79-119.
2018. "Adorno e l'estetica del jazz come *pseudos*", Afterword to Th. W. Adorno, *Variazioni sul jazz. Critica della musica come merce*, trans. by S. Marino, ed. by G. Matteucci, Mimesis, Milano-Udine, pp. 115-143.
2019. *Le verità del non-vero. Tre studi su Adorno, teoria critica ed estetica*, Mimesis, Milano-Udine.

Matteucci G.
2016. "The Aesthetic as a Matter of Practices: Form of Life in Everydayness and Art", in "Comprendre", vol. 18, n. 2, pp. 9-28.
2017. "Everyday Aesthetics and Aestheticization: Reflectivity in Perception", in "Studi di estetica", n. 1, pp. 207-227.
2018. "Il jazz in Adorno: variazioni in serie", Foreword to Th. W. Adorno, *Variazioni sul jazz. Critica della musica come merce*, trans. by S. Marino, ed. by G. Matteucci, Mimesis, Milano-Udine, pp. 7-22.

Maurizi M.
2018. *La vendetta di Dioniso. La musica contemporanea da Schönberg ai Nirvana*, Jaca Book, Milano.

Mecacci A.
2011. *L'estetica del pop*, Donzelli, Roma.
2017. *Dopo Warhol: il pop, il postmoderno, l'estetica diffusa*, Donzelli, Roma.

Middleton R.
1990. *Studying Popular Music*, Open University Press, Milton Keynes-Philadelphia.

Müller-Doohm S.
2005. *Adorno: A Biography*, Polity Press, Cambridge-Malden (MA).

Rognoni L.
1966. *Fenomenologia della musica radicale*, Laterza, Bari.

Salvatore G.
2000. "Introduction" to G. Salvatore (ed.), *Frank Zappa domani. Sussidiario per le scuole (meno) elementari*, Castelvecchi, Roma, pp. 5-16.

Shusterman R.
2000. *Pragmatist Aesthetics: Living Beauty, Rethinking Art* (2nd edition), Rowman & Littlefield, Lanham-Boulder-New York-Oxford.

Tagg P.
2011. *La tonalità di tutti i giorni. Armonia, modalità, tonalità nella popular music. Un manuale*, il Saggiatore, Milano.

Tamm E.
1990. *Robert Fripp: From King Crimson to Guitar Craft*, Faber & Faber, London.

Thorkelson N.
2019. *Herbert Marcuse, Philosopher of Utopia: A Graphic Biography*, City Lights Books, San Francisco.

Vitta M.
2012. *Il rifiuto degli dèi. Teoria delle belle arti industriali*, Einaudi, Torino.

Wellmer A.
2005. "Über Negativität und Autonomie der Kunst. Die Aktualität von Adornos Ästhetik und blinde Flecken seiner Musikphilosophie", in A. Honneth (ed.), *Dialektik der Freiheit. Frankfurter Adorno-Konferenz 2003*, Suhrkamp, Frankfurt a.M., pp. 237-278.

Wilson E.
2003. *Adorned in Dreams: Fashion and Modernity*, I.B. Tauris, London-New York.

Witkin R.
1998. *Adorno on Music*, Routledge, London-New York.
2000. "Why did Adorno 'Hate' Jazz?", in "Sociological Theory", vol. 18, n. 1, pp. 145-170.
2003. *Adorno on Popular Culture*, Routledge, London-New York.

Zurletti S.
2000. "Intervista immaginaria a Theodor Wiesengrund Adorno", in "Nuova rivista musicale italiana", n. 4, pp. 507-514.

Alessandro Alfieri

MINIMALISM AND RAVE MUSIC THROUGH ADORNO
Repetition and Eternal Return of the Same in Contemporary Music

The theoretical tools adopted by Theodor W. Adorno for understanding contemporary art still remain effective today. Adorno died on the eve of a paradigm change between the 1960s and 1970s, but the opposition to neo-avant-gardes arising from Dadaism (like Pop Art) reveals a profound topicality regarding the plastic arts of the last thirty years[1]. Until the end of his career Adorno's philosophy was characterized, among other things, by his remarkable reflections on music. However, if his philosophical contribution was crucial for an adequate understanding of the development of "classical music" or "serious music" from the nineteenth century to the Second Viennese School, it is also true that his writings often appear inadequate to understand the musical phenomena of the post-Webernian age. Indeed, Adorno's references to the Darmstadt School and to *musique concrete* are rare and sporadic, especially if compared to the many references to Schönberg, Berg and Webern, and quite often these references are polemical and unflattering, just as Adorno was very stern also about popular music and jazz, phenomena that undoubtedly marked and still mark the culture of the second half of the twentieth century even beyond specific aesthetic questions.

This essay re-actualizes Adorno's musicological reflection, to retrieve some of the conceptual elements that many philosophers have since adopted to define the dialectical opposition between Schönberg and Stravinsky, and to highlight some problems concerning so much the field of "classic music" and "commercial music". My attention will be focused on American Minimalism,

---

[1] On this topic, see Di Giacomo 2015.

which defined the contemporary music scene since the 1960s and in different ways has continued to influence the collective imaginary until recent times. The development and "destiny" of Minimalism is closely intertwined with that of popular music, leading to immediately to the question the dichotomy between "serious" music and popular music. Several minimalist formal solutions (such as the suppression of the melody, or the insistence on the rhythmic dimension and on repetition) have emerged at the extreme limits of popular music, such as in the techno-dance music of the "rave subculture"[2].

In the *Philosophy of New Music*, Adorno highlighted how, in opposition to Schönberg's dialectical music, Stravinsky opted for a music based on faith in the arrival at an original dimension and an alleged authenticity[3]. Stravinsky's conviction of a polarity between nature and culture is evident in the style of the composer, especially in the operatic works, drawing from origins of music and from dimension of tribal repetition based on constant rhythm, and ignoring historical time. For Adorno, Stravinsky believes that the composer can govern all the musical material of the tradition. In a later essay entitled *Stravinsky. A Dialectical Portrait* Adorno responds to some of the objections raised against him regarding his interpretation of Stravinsky's music, a response which is particularly interesting and fruitful also regarding minimalist music and rave music[4].

In *Stravinsky. A Dialectical Portrait* Adorno offers a more flattering portrait of the composer than the one presented in his *Philosophy of New Music*. On the one side, he specifies here the possibility of interpreting Stravinsky's music in a progressive perspective typical of the Schönberghian style, because the rhythmic repetition of his compositions could indeed express an aesthetically transfigured "truth content": in this way, music points beyond itself, and protests against the eternal repetition of myth. The principle of repetition, transfigured into musical form, could appear then as a critical expression of social reification. This would be the truth content of Stravinskyan music and it would

---

2   See Thornton 1995.
3   See Adorno 2007.
4   See Adorno 1998.

coincide with the denial of subjectivity. On other side, Stravinsky's repetitions and permutations negate the temporality and progression of musical events: they function as kind of "marking time", and this also has implications, of course, for the identity of the subject. Adorno suggests that music must be a transgression of static identity, and therefore opposed to myth, to the immutability of fate and to death itself: "As a temporal art, music is bound to the fact of succession, and is hence as irreversible as time itself. By starting it commits itself to carrying on, to becoming something new, to developing"[5]. The formal error is adopting the static plane of objectivity – the rhythmic session and repetition – thus renouncing development and pretending to give up the temporal dimension. Stravinsky's music is "suffocated", because its sacrifice of the utopian dimension means sacrificing transcendence, and therefore hope and desire for change.

In the following passages, where the incoherence of Stravinsky's music is explained, Adorno's words, also applicable to minimalist music that is structured on rhythmic repetition, are light: "What we may conceive of as musical transcendence, namely, the fact that at any given moment it has become something and something other than it was, that points beyond itself – all that is no mere metaphysical imperative dictated by some external authority. It lies in the nature of music and will not be denied"[6]. But Adorno talks about Stravinsky's mechanical expression as a bad imitation of eternity, reduced to a series of repetitions. It is a "regressive" eternal return as a repetition of the identical, as will happen in Minimalism and in much electronic music. Serial repetition, through the dodecaphonic technique that imposes very strict constraints on the determination of the succession of notes, is a repetition (an initial series that is varied), but it is a "progressive" repetition, an eternal return of the "possibility" rather than of the "same" or the "identical". Adorno says that the same repetition is a scheme of brutalization. The image of deaf-mutism, associated with that of schizophrenia, is useful for understanding the status of passivity that is typical of the conditions of the participants in a rave, where the attempt is to achieve a sensory isolation from the

---

[5] Adorno 1998, pp. 150-151.
[6] Adorno 1998, pp. 150-151.

world. As Simon Reynolds affirms about techno music: "Instead of being a form of self-expression, this is music as *forcefield*, in which the individual is suspended and subjective consciousness is wiped clean away"[7].

The opposition between Stravinsky's and Webern's music is important for the relation between transcendence and repetition; the Webernian law of "contraction" is interpretable as the manifestation of a radical rejection of repetition. The prohibition of repetition and the intensification of the expression coincide with the refusal of extension. Minimalism in figurative arts renounces transcendence, but in minimalist music transcendence is recovered via obsessive repetition, typical of the Buddhist mantra. Repetition is converted from a manifestation of industrial production and of mechanization of the world to an expression of spiritual rituality. The minimalist musicians accused Webern and the whole Second Viennese School of being too abstract but, as Adorno says, Webern's intention was precisely to overcome the sensible in the sensible dimension itself. As in traditional music until the end of the nineteenth century, in Minimalism transcendence is an external character to which the composition yearns, and the Absolute does not "immanentize" itself in the form, determining the process of desensitization of material (as happens exemplarily in Schönberg). Repetition as a way to transcendence is confirmed in the passage from minimalist music to rave music, but in this passage it changes dimension and meaning. The rituality of mantra and exotic tribalism are now transfigured to a postmodern dimension in clandestine parties where drug use and electronic beats' invasiveness appear as renewed forms of orgiastic mystic states.

Several important authors of musical Minimalism come from the Fluxus experience, the neo-avant-garde movement that attempted to overcome art with action (Dadaism) and with the revolution of the everyday (Surrealism). Fluxus theorized and practiced the suppression of the border between art and life. Fluxus included the principal mentor of early Minimalism, John Cage, as well as La Monte Young in his first creative period. Although it started from Fluxus, the results of Minimalist music have travelled very far

---

7   Reynolds 2012, p. 124.

from avant-garde radicalism. The full confluence and confusion of art and life, promoted in his writings by George Maciunas and in the art of Fluxus, is expressed by the intention to overcome the abstract boundary that divides the performer-artist from the spectator, through the adoption of expressive modalities and devices not conventionally specific of traditional arts. This idea of art was replicated in an American artistic scene that subordinated art to market. The art of the German Fluxus group was a critical art, ideologically revolutionary and subversive as Dadaism: for Fluxus and Dadaism, through excess and provocation, the confusion of art and life implied a clear refusal of the rules of marketing.

It is interesting that musical Minimalism, although starting from Fluxus, comes to conceive the overcoming of art and life in a diametrically opposed direction to Cage, Volstell or June Paik, and it is for this reason that minimalist visual arts and Minimalist music diverge considerably. Minimalist art, as Fluxus, belongs to the modern tradition that began with Dadaism, while Minimalist music, also strongly influenced by this tradition, is definitely closer to the sensibility and the aesthetics of Pop (which is, however, also heir to Dadaist aesthetics). Michael Nyman, one of the second-generation minimalist composers, says about the relationship between Minimalism and Fluxus:

> Perhaps a reaction against indeterminacy was inevitable: the music of La Monte Young and Terry Riley, Steve Reich and Philip Glass – the three other American composers most closely associated with Young's minimal "alternative" – shows a many-sided retrenchment from the music that has grown from indeterminacy, and draws on sources hitherto neglected by experimental music. This music not only cuts down the area of sound-activity of an absolute (and absolutist) minimum, but submits the scrupulously selective, mainly tonal, material to mostly repetitive, highly disciplined procedures which are focused with an extremely fine definition (though the listener's focusing is not done for him).[8]

The Minimalist movement of American composers was born with the intention of opposing European experimental music and refusing the extreme developments of serial music. In the

---

8   Nyman 2009, p. 139.

field of music, the minimalists rejected the cerebral complexity of serial music that dominated the European scene after the Second World War, in order to promote a return to the tonality with most elementary forms: harmonic movements reduced to a minimum, and repetitions in "obstinate" of rhythmic patterns and small melodic diatonic elements[9]. Philip Glass's words are exemplary of this severity towards European avant-garde music, which he defined, "a wasteland, dominated by these maniacs, these creeps, who were trying to make everyone write this crazy creepy music"[10].

Through the use of magnetic tape, the European music of the Darmstadt School challenged and destroyed the little that had survived in terms of melody and enjoyment of listening: for the capacity of judgment of American musicians the result was a music exaggeratedly cerebral, far from any more elementary condition of listening and taste, elitist and "unlistenable". Adorno had by this time expressed his perplexity about that kind of new European music, but his reasons were distant from those of the minimalists. For Adorno it was an abjuration of the principle of formal configuration, and a renunciation of any temporality and development within the musical work, and was thus condemned to the impossibility of expressing any critical-dialectical content against the world and the society. The denial of the internal temporality of the work of art means the exclusion of any evolution and goes against the real concept of music.

The will of the Minimalists was instead to bring the masses closer to "classical music", in opposition to the Adornian dichotomy of high culture and popular culture; emerging from absolute abstraction, numerous minimalist experiences started from popular music or end there. While in the figurative arts it was minimalism that influenced Pop Art, in music it was, vice-versa, pop music that triggered a certain influence on musical Minimalism. The formal and stylistic operation that Minimalism has adopted since the 1960s denies the achievements of modern and serial music. Minimalism rather wants to adopt the principle of repetition and serialization to put it at the service of the return of rhythm and harmony.

---

9   See Károlyi 1996.
10 Glass, quoted in Ross 2007, p. 378.

In order to understand these problems, it is necessary to return to the radical distinction between minimalist plastic arts and musical Minimalism. Serialization is the typical prerogative of modernity, and above all of post-modernity: the new avant-gardes and the industrial production are based on serialization, and so are phenomena such as the Neo-Pop that adhere to the full overlap of the two dimensions. Even the Minimalism of Robert Morris and Richard Serra relies on the principle of serialization, creating installations and "environments" characterized by essential objects reduced to their material consistency, repeated indefinitely. Often these are industrial materials without aesthetic appearance, decorative quality or expressiveness. The principle that underlies this art is well summarized by the words of one of its protagonists, Donald Judd: "putting one thing after another" in a maniacal and compulsive manner, suppressing every aesthetical dimension. In music this serialization becomes something different: the hypnotic repetition of compositional patterns does not happen in a random way, but in a well-considered way, with an attention for the listener's taste that had been completely compromised in modern European music. The postmodern popular taste unquestionably appreciates the obsessive seriality, because as the characterizing principle of techno and rave music "the intensity of the excitement grows as the listener indulges in motor induction and it is directly proportional to the repetition of a given rhythmic sequence, so that, instead of weakening, it increases thanks to repetition"[11].

As we have seen, the repetition that characterizes musical Minimalism could be a mere reflection of the current condition of post-industrial society – as an eternal return of the "same", a form of infernal time of market and fashion because fashion does not interrupt the new but rather means the eternal return of the new, thus meaning a "return of the same". But paradoxically, in the same time, this music assumes a truthful character inasmuch as it is able to release a critical value precisely in relation to reality – as an eternal return of the "possible", a repetition as a condition of possibility of differences and of the new. The second position seems adequate to Minimalism in the plastic arts, because in that case Minimalism is a critical parody of the serialization of industrial production. In

---

[11] Cano and Battistini 2015, p. 63 (my transl.).

musical Minimalism this repetition of the "same" can become a tool to allow the adherence of art to the mechanisms of production through taste. For Robert Fink Minimalist music is a critical music, where repetition takes a progressive meaning; Minimalism takes on a polemic role against late capitalism, because the excess of repetition that characterizes the consumer society is a repetition that sacrifices meaning, while minimalist production is opposed to consumption through a different conception of repetition – a repetition that is different from the seriality of Pop Art, where serial repetitions are not against massive consumption, but they are more intended to bring together artistic dimension and culture industry:

> A culture of repetition arises when the extremely high level of repetitive structuring necessary to sustain capitalist modernity becomes salient in its own right, experienced directly as constituent of subjectivity; it is in this sense that we are constantly "repeating ourselves", fashioning and regulating our lived selves through manifold experiences of repetition. "Pure" control of/by repetition has become a familiar yet unacknowledged aesthetic effect of late modernity, sometimes experienced as pleasurable and erotic, but more often as painfully excessive, alienating, and (thus) sublime.[12]

If the repetition of the "same", which characterizes the industrial production and the society of the spectacle, is a repetition based on a death instinct, the minimalist aesthetic repetition is not a repetition of "identical elements" but would rather refer to "Eros". For this reason, for Fink, it is possible to recognize in our society a culture of Eros for which repetition is creation of desire, and both Steve Reich's music and remixes of the disco music tracks do the same "cultural action" as two aspects of the same phenomenon. Dance music would highlight the libidinal essence of rhythm, already insistent in Minimalism but explicit and disruptive in the disco itself. Minimalism, according to this interpretation, is therefore an effective cultural practice and not a symptom of a social pathology. In Minimalist composers the concept of repetition assumes a great complexity, a repetition that is not "repetition of the same" but "repetition of the rhythmic force": the

---

[12] Fink 2005, p. 4.

rhythmic series of a composer as Reich adopt numerous variations of the dominant series.

The accusation that minimalist music is an anti-teleological music because it lacks development and an authentically temporal structure (what Adorno said about Stravinsky's music) is rejected by Fink, who believes that it is not legitimate to distinguish a teleological music from an anti-teleological one: Minimalism, renouncing mimicry of the orgasm by excluding the formal development of the composition, offers a "non-teleological jouissance" interpretable as a state of ecstasy. The plane of ecstasy is in fact the minimalist attempt to restore the value of transcendence, which is recovered in the rhythmic obsession. It is precisely in focusing on "non-teleological jouissance" that we can rediscover a continuity between Minimalism and rave subculture, which precisely in the collective ecstasy traces an opportunity to escape from the world. On the other hand, the degeneration of minimalist music has been highlighted by Wim Mertens, who is an important composer but also an Adornian theorist, and Fink himself refers to him when he speaks about the anti-dialectical, politically retrograde and psychologically regressive tendency that has also appeared in Minimalism.

Minimalism, especially since the late 1970s and strongly in the 1980s, has definitely become mainstream through musicians such as Wim Mertens, Brian Eno, Michael Nyman. This music merged into popular music fully translating repetitive minimalist aspects into Pop series, inasmuch as repetition itself, in the late capitalist consumerist universe, lends itself perfectly to the cultural market. Minimalist research has since then been technically and expressively received by numerous trends in popular culture, such as hip-hop and drone music, and through some mediating figures such as Carsten Nicolai (aka Alva Noto) and Richie Hawtin, minimalist music has appeared in the characteristic genres of the rave subculture: "In techno music, in a diachronic sense, there is no linear sequence, with a beginning and an end, but rather a circular sequence; the feeling is that of an 'eternal present'. Similarly, in a synchronic sense, techno is not made up of a single melodic line, more or less elaborate, but rather of multiple sound lines, not always parallel, which often intersect themselves"[13].

---

13   Cano and Battistini 2015, p. 58 (my transl.).

It is not difficult to find attempts to rehabilitate rave music, understood as a tendency for opposing rules that stiffen the world, but there is no doubt that the "eternal present" of rhythmic construction is opposed to that which for Adorno is the duty of music: "preserving the forgotten", in contrast to the absolute removal of the past in rave music. The hypnotic and suffocating "mechanical complexity" of Stravinsky's music, an effective reflection of the schizophrenia of the individual in the era of late capitalism, could be interpreted in terms of a complaint to the same social order that exists in the administered world. This is what we could presumably also say about Minimalism, both plastic and musical, on the basis of Fink's theory, especially music, which is the "art of time" that cannot deny "becoming". The adoption of the absolute hedonistic dimension is fully accomplished with rave culture, which makes of the repetition of the "same" and identity the constitutive principles and the dominant logical matrix: "Becoming a mass phenomenon, the rave is therefore characterized by the choice of being outside the official local circuits, outside the "commercial" music, outside a controlled and regulated concept of entertainment. But progressively the spread of rave also attracts the cultural industry [...] from the original idea of parade, also as a protest, we move towards an increasingly hedonistic perspective"[14].

For Adorno, Stravinsky's limitation was a lack of an ethical and utopian dimension in his music. Showing the brutality of the suppression of the individual, through the projection in a mythical past, the composer did not propose, even negatively, a dimension of redemption and transformation, which music itself should express through development. This is what we also find in Minimalism, which renounces any structural principle and any development, limiting itself to a maniacal repetition that indefinitely reflects itself without proposing any opportunity for change. In this way, through the loss of any transcendence understood as a utopian and revolutionary value, Minimalist repetitive music presents itself uniquely and tautologically without bringing up any condition of new possibility. This repetition, freed from the constraints of transcendence of the "truth content", perfectly adheres to the principle of enjoyment that this music claims for itself.

---

14   Cano and Battistini 2015, p. 44 (my transl.).

If organizing music musically means transcending it, there is no doubt that the harbingers of the degeneration of music from the art of time to the art of immobility can already be traced in Minimalist music. Once the principle of transcendence – which for Adorno was offered in Beethoven outside the formal structure (the Absolute as "over"), while in Schönberg it was immanent in formal desensitization (the Absolute as the silence of formal fragmentation), and which coincides with the utopian value of their music – was lost, then minimalist composers often tried to recover this dimension of transcendence in oriental cults. Obsessive repetition is the *mantra*, which seeks the Absolute (*Nirvana*) precisely in the eternal cyclic nature of the same formulas repeated until exhaustion, and the same holds true for other musicians who let themselves be deeply influenced by indigenous cults and African tribal traditions. This "mystical" level of recovery of transcendence is translated into rave culture in the consumption of "ecstasy", as a rite of initiation and adherence to the group: "this was the Dionysian paroxysm programmed and looped for eternity"[15], and for this reason several interpreters have traced a link between religious practices and raves[16].

Adorno would argue that those who interpret rave music in a "progressive" or emancipatory sense underestimate the formal-artistic specificities of this genre: on the one hand, "[...] the rave does not seem to emerge, as opposed to what is sometimes written, as a space of solitude and non-communication [but] conveys a new utopia, that of non-verbal communication"[17]; on the other hand, this type of utopia immediately reveals its illusory nature because its mode of expression denies development and therefore transformation, evolution, difference. We can highlight a further point of consonance between Stravinsky and the first Minimalist music, and then rave music: the matter of confirming the tribal dimension, represented by the absolute value covered by the rhythmic session, also in the electro-technological production of contemporary music which replaces mantra with the computer's loop of beats.

---

15 Reynolds 2012, p. 16.
16 See St. John et al. 2004.
17 Cano and Battistini 2015, p. 58 (my transl.).

As we said, Minimalism arrived in the 1980s and 1990s in music linked to urban subcultures, such as techno-dance and techno-minimal, the genres of rave culture. Techno music is characterized by elementary rhythms formed by bass and percussion of electronic sonority, where any harmonic or melodic principle is absent. The essentiality of the rhythmic elements is a further simplification with respect to Minimalism; particularly suggestive is that the mythical dimension and the cultic primitivism characteristic of Minimalism have been translated into the culture of the rave and techno music. The primitivism of Stravinsky's music and jazz is viewed with suspicion by Adorno as a symptom of the regression of listening and an expression of the mythical tendencies of collective subjugation, and the rave represents a postmodern translation of this primitivistic regression. The subject of the rave is a "We" which is a reflection of exclusive isolation; it coincides with the suppression of the individual, who, rather than trying to affirm him- or herself, prefers to disperse in the identity itself within the perpetuated identity of contemporary culture. Comparing techno music with the other epigone of Minimalism represented by popular music in the strict sense, we can see that the same conclusions are reached in different ways: on the one hand, "techno music [...] does not know this dualism melody/accompaniment or verse/refrain; there is no such clear beginning and end, and repetition and overlapping of sound tracks emerge and sink freely"[18]; on the other hand, popular music represents full adherence to the laws of the market, and as Adorno claims the adoption of plugging or standardization of listening involves tested formulas that are repeated incessantly, that guarantee familiarity and therefore enjoyment to the listener.

In conclusion, we have to remember how Adorno, in his controversial articulation of the most radical results of post-war serial music, had already rejected a conception of absolute technical rigor of the composition; indeed the mathematical modalities of composition completely suffocate the subjective dimension, bringing to a non-dialectical extreme dodecaphony's intention that through geometric rigidity one could still guarantee an ethical and critical perspective towards the world. In order to

---

18   Cano and Battistini 2015, p. 58 (my transl.).

recover the value of the subject, dissolved during a gradual process, music needs to evade reduction to an absolute mechanical process which reflects the world uncritically. From the cult of minimalist anti-teleological repetition – which sought transcendence after having denied it – passing to the second minimalist generation, which brings its technical results to commercial music and popular music, replacing the pursuit of transcendence with the principle of enjoyment proper to massification – to the typical techno and dance music of the rave subculture, where the subject has completely vanished in a dimension of collective ecstasy favored by the consumption of drugs and the environment, as well as by a music that is based exclusively on rhythm, which does not show melodic structures nor temporal constructions nor developments. As Philip Tagg affirms, techno music renounces the meaning and the individual "Figure" to affirm a dominance of the general identity of the "Ground", devoid of any element of redemption because it is based on a temporality that is not a "becoming" but a cyclical, static status. But Tagg himself asks a question to which he himself does not answer:

> Bearing in mind that real rave credibility consists of anonymously recording tracks on white labels, is it possible to suggest that the non-individualist character of the music actually does express a rejection of degenerate, hegemonic notions of the individual? Bearing also in mind the often semi-illegal, cooperative way in which raves are organized, is it going too far to hypothesize that rave music prefigures new forms of collective consciousness? Or are rave organizers another variation on the old "hip capitalist" theme and rave DJs a mere variation on the old theme of central figure against general background?[19]

Adorno himself seems, with the next words, to provide an answer to Tagg's question:

> It is true that some of the bodily functions, which the individual has really lost, are imaginatively returned to him by music. Yet this is but half the truth: in the mechanical rigor of their repetition, the functions copied by the rhythm are themselves identical with

---

19   Tagg 1994, p. 219.

those of the production process which robbed the individual of his original bodily functions. The function of music is ideological not only because it hoodwinks people with an irrationality that allegedly has no power over the discipline of their existence. It is ideological also because it makes that irrationality resemble the models of rationalized labor.[20]

Bibliography

Adorno Th. W.
1976. *Introduction to the Sociology of Music*, Seabury Press, New York, 1976.
1998. "Stravinsky: A Dialectical Portrait", in *Quasi una fantasia: Essays on Modern Music*, trans. by R. Livingstone, Verso, New York.
2007. *Philosophy of New Music*, trans. by A.G. Mitchell and W.V. Blomster, Continuum, London-New York.

Cano C. and Battistini E.
2015. *Musica e cinema nel dopoguerra americano*, Gremese, Roma.

Di Giacomo G.
2015. *Fuori dagli schemi. Estetica e arti figurative dal Novecento a oggi*, Laterza, Roma-Bari.

Fink R.
2005. *Repeating ourselves. American minimal music as cultural practice*, University of California Press, Los Angeles-London.

Károlyi O.
1996. *Modern American Music: From Charles Ives to the Minimalists*, Diane Publishing Co., Darby (PA).

Nyman M.
2009. *Experimental Music. Cage and beyond*, Cambridge University Press, London-New York.

Reynolds S.
2012. *Energy Flash. A journey through rave music and dance culture*, Soft Skull Press, Berkeley (CA).

---

20   Adorno 1976, p. 52.

Ross A.
2007. *The rest is noise. Listening to the twentieth Century*, Picador, New York.

St John G. et al.
2004. *Rave Culture and Religion*, Routledge, New York.

Tagg P.
1994. "From Refrain to Rave. The Decline of Figure and the Rise of Ground", in "Popular Music", vol. 13, n. 2.

Thornton S.
1995. *Club Cultures: Music, Media, and Subcultural Capital*, Wesleyan University Press, Middletown (CT).

Giacomo Fronzi

THEODOR W. ADORNO DEFENDER OF POP MUSIC, *MALGRÉ LUI*

1. Introduction

From whatever perspective Theodor W. Adorno's thought is analyzed, interpreted and criticized, it shows specific characteristics that make it unique in the philosophical landscape of the twentieth century. One could argue that one does not find a philosopher, understood in the full sense of the term, if one does not find an original and different reflection from the others. Nevertheless, some intellectuals demonstrate radical uniqueness on the basis of what we could define as a "multi-level originality". Conceptual articulation, language, writing style, combination of different cultural planes, research interests: on each of these levels, Adorno has manifested a specificity such as to make his philosophy effectively unique in the context of twentieth-century thinking.

Within this general framework, one must bear in mind that Adornian philosophy has expressed itself in a powerfully new way within a field of study that is probably born and, in some ways, dies with it: the philosophy of music. Beyond the provocation, it would be more correct to say that there was no trace, after 1969, of a philosophy of music like that of Adorno. We could then say that there is the philosophy of music and the philosophy of music "*sub specie* Adorniana", referring with this expression to that very particular synthesis of theoretical philosophy, philosophy of history, musicology, sociology and compositional analysis that only Adorno was able to produce.

In this essay, I will try to retrace Adornian thought in relation to popular music, to try to demonstrate how, *malgré lui*, the philosopher from Frankfurt, criticizing this sector of music production, anticipated forms of popular music with a connotation that he himself would have considered positive, in terms of the treatment of musical material and the relationship with the historical-social moment. To do this, however, it is necessary to proceed step by step, starting from the relationship between music and mass society and the concept of "musical material", and then move on to the criticism of pop music and its unexpected redress.

2. Between Philosophy and Sociology

Adorno's philosophical thought immediately wore the "musicological" guise. In the legendary Institut für Sozialforschung in Frankfurt am Main, founded in 1922, there are those who deal with Philosophy (Max Horkheimer and Herbert Marcuse), with Economics (Henryk Grossmann), with Literature (Leo Löwenthal) and with Music (Adorno). This means that the relationship between philosophical articulation, musical analysis and criticism of society has always represented, for the philosopher from Frankfurt, the horizon within which to move. Hence, his interest in fundamental issues: listening, the relationship between music and radio reproduction (or, in a more general sense, between music and technique), the relationships between musical developments and economic-social developments, the complex question of what the functions of art and (serious) music can be, in a society of late or advanced capitalism.

Therefore, the continuous dialogue between a plan that we could define as "philosophy of history" and that more specifically of "philosophy of music" is central for Adorno. This leads us to focus our attention on how music and (mass) society relate, what results (positive and negative) emerge and how both can (or should) influence each other. In particular, throughout his life, Adorno analyzes the work of composers such as Beethoven, Mahler, Schönberg, Berg, Webern and Strauss in which he sees a specific interweaving between the political-social dimension and the compositional dimension itself, such as to become a paradigm of the different moments of development of European society between the nineteenth and twentieth century. After all, the criticism articulated by Adorno points straight to the heart of bourgeois aesthetics, guilty of having gradually and inexorably overcome (or destroyed) the combination between these two dimensions. But, as Peter Hohendhal argued, "this necessary defense of the social and thereby political character of the artwork speaks more to the configuration of the early 20th century. It would be hermeneutically implausible to ignore this distance and treat Adorno's text and the nature of its intervention as direct responses to the postmodern condition of the late twentieth century"[1].

But this is not the subject of this essay, and we can put aside the analysis of the composers mentioned above to focus on the specific relationship between musical work, history and society, underlining once again how, in Adorno, philosophy of music, philosophy of history and sociology tend to coincide.

Adorno was well aware of the fact that, wanting to establish a constant relationship (at times of correspondence at others of opposition) between music and society, he could not escape the confrontation with the sociology of music[2]: on it depends both the analysis of cultured music and that of popular music. Here it should be made clear that Adorno's opinion with respect to sociology understood as empirical research is decidedly critical and starts from the assumption that the fact that there are certain disciplines and forms of thought is not sufficient to justify their existence[3]. When we talk about "sociology", says Adorno, we refer to types of analysis that are categorized together in an abstract sense, just because they refer generically to society. In reality, they are not unitary either in terms of their object or their method: some look at the social totality and its dynamic laws, while others address specific social phenomena that do not refer to a unitary concept of society. Changing the object of analysis also changes the method that, by analogy with a specific trend of empirical sociology for which what is primary becomes secondary (the epiphenomenon is mistaken for the thing itself), leads to the prevalence of methodological issues over those content. By virtue of these aspects, many empirical studies show an evident irrelevance[4].

---

1   Hohendhal 1992, p. 15.
2   Adorno 2012.
3   Adorno 1957.
4   Adorno 1957.

Starting from these premises, Adorno's analyses are at the same time something more and something less than pure and simple sociological investigations. They are something less to the extent that one cannot speak, strictly speaking, of sociological research, since the relationship with empirical sociology is completely marginal, just as there is absolutely no attempt to rigorously parametrize the various degrees or levels of representation of the diffusion, presence or absence of a given object of investigation in society. They are, however, something more because they present themselves as a musical sociology in which music means more than cigarettes or soap in market surveys and which must be aware of society and its structure, have a precise knowledge of musical phenomena, but, above all, should understand music itself in all its implications[5]. Adorno points out that the relationship of correspondence between artistic construction and social totality should not be considered in terms of "structural homology": his analysis does not reveal a correspondence between different planes, but rather a mutual clarification between elements so constitutionally intertwined as to make it impossible to separate them. This observation is connected to the "double character" of art[6], i.e. its being autonomous and, at the same time, *fait social*. The difference that is created, from a sociological point of view, involves the differentiation between two levels that are *not complementary*: an internal level, which gives rise to a "sociology of the musical object" (for which music is analyzed "in itself", with its own original and immanent meaning, with its own internal articulations), and an external level, which gives rise to a "sociology of the musical function" (which is responsible for studying the dynamics and characteristics of the modifications made in the process of functionalization of the musical object, that is, when the work has been assigned a function of entertainment, escape, etc.)[7].

Even compared to what we said at the beginning, the Adornian contributions of "sociology of the object" (those dedicated, for example, to Mahler, Wagner, Schönberg, Stravinsky, Beethoven, etc.) are actually less numerous than those of "sociology of

---

5   Adorno 1957.
6   Adorno 2002a, p. 3.
7   Adorno 1959.

function". However, the lack of complementarity of the two approaches is cannot be properly configured as a methodological or procedural dualism; it is rather a differentiation of objects of investigation. Thus, "the root of the separation between "sociology of function" and "sociology of the object" is to be found in Adorno's *dualistic* conception of musical facts, which leads to the creation of two fields of objects qualified by opposite characteristics: the being-in-itself of musical facts is a way of being that excludes their functionality, and vice versa"[8]. Musical works that keep their distance from existence, from social relations of production, that assume the status of "monades", are guaranteed their positive and truthful value (cultured music, even if not all and not as such). At the other end of the spectrum are non-autonomous works, for which the lack of isolation causes their possible or potential content of truth to disappear (pop music or jazz). In this perspective, the "sociology of the object" is the method of analysis of the authentic, while the "sociology of function" is the method of demystification of the inauthentic[9].

This is where the question of the social critique of radio music and the critique of pop music comes in, which we will arrive at not before having inserted a necessary *Mittelglied*, since it is exactly the point of conjunction between the compositional-creative level and the historical-social level: the musical material.

3. The Musical Material (and the Form)

The concept of "material" is central to Adorno's thought and has been present in his production since the 1930s. However, this centrality is not matched by a precise definition, thus giving rise to different interpretations. Meanwhile, the musical material is to be understood as something irreducible to the set of technical-formal possibilities inscribed in an a-historical and a-temporal horizon. Instead, it is placed in a dynamic in which it is a central element for the definition of every moment of the history of musical progress, both in its strictly technical and in its social version. The material

---

8 Serravezza 1976, p. 81.
9 Serravezza 1976, p. 93.

therefore has a historical and social character that Adorno uses as a parameter to assess the degree of authenticity of a composer and the content of truth of a work is "a concept that, in relation to the specific 'historical complication', ends up offering itself as an essential reference for the investigation of the 'truth content' of the work"[10]. It is a free action of the composer, who operates in a precise historical-social framework and in the interweaving of the contradictions that characterize it. The composer's freedom lies in the choice of techniques (which are also historically determined), in the definition of his own poetics and in his own sensitivity, even though he is in any case limited. The progressive composer is the one who manages to grasp the musical material at the most advanced level of his historical dialectic.

Therefore, the musical material is an external instance in which history and spirit are sedimented, which acts on the work, conditioning the process of construction. It is a "passive heritage" that reaches artists under the pressure of tradition and, at the same time, a source of "active coercion" on the artists themselves. The material, if captured to the maximum degree of its historical dialectics, translates the sedimented history and the sedimented spirit into music; this means that the material, being an anonymous and abstract instance, contrasts in some way with the individual and concrete work of art in which it nevertheless manifests itself. Max Paddison also refers to this differentiation in tackling this theme, distinguishing between the immanent dialectic and the social dialectic of the musical material[11]. Paddison recalls how for Adorno "material" should not be considered only in the sense of "raw material" (*Stoff*), and consequently only as what is forged during the compositional process of a work. The musical material is in itself historically "pre-formed": "That is to say, musical material is mediated not only because it is shaped, more or less consistently, within the form of the work itself, but precisely because it is already historically and culturally pre-formed before any individual act of composition even begins"[12]. This means that the musical material pre-exists, culturally and historically, the work

---

10   Arbo 1991, p. 112.
11   See Paddison 1993.
12   Paddison 1993, p. 149.

and to the compositional act. However, Paddison continues, from these considerations a basic ambiguity emerges Adorno seems to emphasize the general concept of "material" with respect to the more specific and particular concept of the musical work. It is in the "progress of musical material" that he sees a manifestation of the "progress of the spirit" and not within the individual musical work. At the same time, Adorno suggests that the general progress of the material can only be achieved through its manifestation in particular works. This ambiguity, Paddison argues, can perhaps be overcome through the analysis of the concept of form[13], which is also particularly obscure, because it is used in two different ways, albeit connected: "form at the level of the pre-formed musical material, and form at the level of the individual musical work. The aim here is twofold: to examine the relationship between these two levels of form, as the mediation of universal and particular, and to consider the problem of formal integration in relation to what he sees as the disintegration of musical material"[14].

The concept of "form" in Adorno refers to the sum of all the moments of logic and coherence of an artwork. In the critical (that is to say, formal) elaboration of its various moments, art is placed dialectically and conflictually at the opposite pole to the empirical reality, whose elements are given a non-empirical concept: "Form works like a magnet that orders elements of the empirical world in such a fashion that they are estranged from their extra-aesthetic existence, and it is only as a result of this estrangement that they master the extra-aesthetic essence"[15].

What happens if we relate this definition of form to that of musical material understood as something that is already "pre-formed"? On the one hand, in the pre-formed material there is already some meaning, "in the sense of culturally shared understanding of socially and historically mediated aesthetic norms and conventions"[16]. From this more general point of view, the form should be considered as an essential and fundamental attribute of the material, because, as we said, the material is

---

13 Bruns 2008.
14 Paddison 1993, p. 149.
15 Adorno 2002a, p. 226.
16 Paddison 1993, p. 150.

already "formed" and therefore not "natural". Paddison goes on to say that, on the other hand, however, these conventional meanings (figurations, formulas, etc.) are dismantled, deconstructed and recontextualized in a new complex of meanings that is represented by the "immanent law of form" of each specific musical work. From this more particular point of view, form should not be considered as a fundamental attribute of the material, but the organization and recontextualization "of the historically available 'layers' of material to give them new meaning at the level of the individual composition. It is in the field of tension between these two levels that he appears to locate the 'truth content' of a work: the consistency of its immanent form in relation to the divergent socio-historical tendency of its pre-formed material"[17].

If there are deep relationships between the two concepts of form and material, focusing on the latter, it is possible to proceed with the definition of some of its essential characters. According to Sara Zurletti, four qualities should be examined[18].

The first is *arbitrariness*, an aspect linked to the selective nature of the material. It is not a necessary device, which arbitrarily selects sound combinations in the infinite mass of possible sound combinations, forcing the composer and the listener to refer only to them. From this point of view, the material functions as a language: it arbitrarily divides and articulates the flow of experience, and then imposes on the speakers the use of the result.

Being an arbitrary construction, the musical material depends on a sort of consensus that is established among musicians and listeners and that guarantees its validity, manifesting its *social character* (second quality). It is this mechanism that, for example, has allowed (and still allows) the tonal system to remain, even if in a weakened form, stable over the centuries. The material, like the tonal system and linguistic codes, is born to circulate in society, it is taken up again, elaborated, modified, evolves and is able to keep alive precisely because of these constant adaptations. It is a mediation under a double aspect: it is an intermediate term between "social immediacy" and "artwork", but it is also an intermediate term between "individual composer" and "society", guaranteeing a flow

---

17   Paddison 1993, p. 150.
18   See Zurletti 2006.

of communication between the two subjects. The musical material is a device that is common to all members of the community and exercises a function of "universal communication", just like the linguistic codes. As such, musical material also has a *constricting function* (third quality) that it exerts on composers and listeners as do linguistic codes on speakers.

The fourth quality has to do with the *historical character* of the material, which, albeit temporarily, escapes the possibility of being modified by the individual, in whose hands it arrives, as we have said, already pre-formed. The freedom that the musician expresses is, initially, circumscribed by the material. However, this "inalterability" is only partial, since the material is "continuously altered": it could only be expressed through a more or less subversive act of the composer. The "subversive" attempts can have transforming effects only with the passing of time, in the interactions with other attempts. Only after a process of this nature can the changes be absorbed into the code and there will be, consequently, a structural innovation. The material is therefore subject to innovation and change, in line with a vision, as is the Adornian one, of the teleological evolution of music, which makes musical progress irreversible. According to Adorno, in fact, music is a temporal art and, as such, is linked to the form of succession through its pure *medium*. For this reason, it is irreversible as time is irreversible[19]. Precisely because of this idea of progressivity, the material functions as an evaluation criterion, as a sort of "gradient of evolution". For Adorno, as we shall see, the last stage of development of music is represented by the *neue Musik*, which reaches the maximum degree of rationalization of the musical means and the overcoming of the tonal system, no longer able to absorb in itself the contradictions and lacerations of the world, in a perspective of radical criticism of society. These aspects, which Adorno considers completely absent in the field of jazz and popular music, as we shall see, will appear just where the philosopher from Frankfurt did not imagine he could find them.

It is evident that the musical material has a central role not only in the philosophical analysis of the evolutionary processes of music but also from a sociological point of view of music. As Paddison

---

19   Adorno 1963.

suggests, in fact, alongside the immanent dialectic of musical material, there is also a *social dialectic*, which is to be understood as the antagonistic relationship between aesthetic forces and production relations (such as the composer's relationship with the musical material) and material relations of production (such as the relationship of the cultural industry with the musical work). In this context, there is the split between the autonomy of the work of art and its inevitable sliding into the dynamics of commodification, which would exclude popular music from the list of potentially valid and acceptable music (according to Adorno's categories). As will be seen, for Adorno the separation of the latter, as we will see, implies its inevitable assimilation into the gears of the cultural industry. This dynamic demonstrates the fact that the musical material reflects and reproduces the model of production-reproduction-distribution-consumption. As an internal element in the dialectic of musical material, the composer, as a creative subject, is not a tabula rasa but is, as is musical material, culturally and socially mediated. Adorno does not consider the concepts of "creativity", "spontaneity", "inspiration" or "free play" to be of particular use. What is crucial in the realization of great music is the way in which the composer responds to the needs of the material: "In this way the composer's subjectivity, as spontaneity, serves to mediate the contradictions of the material, contradictions which are themselves social and historical in origin"[20]. It is essentially a process of rationalization involving both the composer and the musical material. Thus, through the emphasis on the rationalization process (especially as technical and technological development) as an important factor in the mediation of musical material and society, Adorno comes to believe that the interaction of the composer with the musical material is at the same time the interaction with society, but only to the extent that this interaction is expressed exclusively in the musical work. As we have already said, for Adorno the relationship between composer and society is to be understood as a response to the needs of the musical material. And it is completely irrelevant whether or not composers are aware of "social tendencies".

---

20   Paddison 1993, p. 188.

What has been said so far, in relation to the relationship between music and society and musical material, refers to the dichotomy by virtue of which music can be serious (if it resists its destiny as a commodity, is at the highest level of awareness of the development of musical material, if it has a critical function, if it expresses a truth content) or it cannot be so (if it proves not to have the requisites of serious music). This macro-distinction corresponds to the distinction between classical and popular music, even though Adorno also identifies composers and works within classical music that are not up to the function and role of art in the advanced capitalist society. According to Paddison, in Adorno "serious" and "popular" music should be considered as two complementary halves of a single complex. The division is not between serious and popular as such, as this division has become less and less significant due to an increasingly pervasive cultural industry, but "is much more between, on the one hand, music which accepts its character as commodity, thus becoming identical with the machinations of the culture industry itself, and, on the other hand, that self-reflective music which critically opposes its fate as commodity, and thus ends up by alienating itself from present society by becoming unacceptable to it"[21].

On closer inspection, Adorno does not condemn the whole of non-serious music *tout court*, so much so as he himself brings the distinction between classical and light music back to the barbaric position it came from[22]. Music production is extremely differentiated. Serious music, to use Adorno's expression, has a specific tradition, structure and content, not comparable with other musical experiences. From this depends a distinction of value that, in any case, must be made, since it is typical of any critical analysis. Consequently, however negative the operation of Adorno's hierarchy may seem, it appears legitimate. *Distingue frequenter*. And the distinction that Adorno makes (and that can only follow a comparison) is that between "good music" and "bad music", thus leaving open (and widely practicable) the path of bad music even within serious music. In fact, in the essay on popular music (and in many other places) Adorno will have no difficulty in

---

21 Paddison 1982, p. 204.
22 Adorno 1953.

criticizing the existence of "bad serious music"; it comes down to assessing the relationship between the music in question and the "system". According to Adorno, "the organization of culture into 'levels' such as the first, second and third programs, patterned after low, middle and highbrow, is reprehensible"[23]. Undoubtedly, however, Adorno's point of view does not include good music that is not serious. On the one hand, therefore, Adorno's preference for some composers and not others, for a certain kind of musical work over others, is linked to the need to analyze models that embody a precise theoretical perspective or that, on the contrary, distance themselves from it. On the other hand, the fact of not taking into account the possibility that good popular music may exist leads us to have to question the basis of the considerations that the philosopher seems to want to relegate *all* popular music to the category of pure merchandise, apparently without giving it any chance of salvation.

4. Against Pop Music

In 1941, Adorno published the famous essay "On Popular Music"[24], thus becoming the first theorist of popular music (broadcast by radio). In these pages, some theses already presented in the essay "Über den Fetischcharakter in der Musik und die Regression des Hörens" (1938)[25] and then in "A Social Critique of Radio Music" (1945), such as those of standardization and structural banality, repetitiveness, regression of listening, pseudo-individualization, etc., return. However, there are also considerable insights, starting from the questions related to a basic question: what is popular music? Adorno does not provide a precise definition, nor does he refer to a single musical genre (light music, folk, dance, etc.). Paddison points out how surprising such a lack of differentiation is in a philosopher who, in the field of serious music, constantly insists on the need to make a distinction. Paddison's explanation is that "Adorno simply detested popular music, and in assessing

---

23   Adorno 1983, p. 127.
24   Adorno 2002c.
25   Adorno 2002b.

it was content to give way to his own irrational prejudices in the most uncritical and unreflective manner"[26]. We could then say that popular music is defined by its difference from serious music, a difference that is placed on different levels despite their dependence on each other. As always, as we said at the beginning, these are both strictly musical and social issues, starting with the first fundamental characteristic of popular music: *standardization*.

According to Adorno, the structure of popular music tracks is standardized at all levels, even when trying to circumvent that standardization. The proof is the fact that the most common rule in popular music is the use of a chorus of thirty-two bars and that the extension (range) is limited to one octave and one note[27]. Standardization characterizes not only the structure but also the details, contrary to what happens in serious music: in Beethoven, for example, every detail receives musical sense from the concrete totality of the work, just as, on the contrary, the work lives on the relationship between all the details and never depends on the simple application of a scheme. The part-whole-relationship is absent in popular music pieces, in which it is possible to replace or eliminate details without having particular consequences on the musical sense. It is then evident that the relationship between details and totality is completely accidental and that the structure is only "a mere musical automatism"[28]. It is not a question, however, of contrasting popular music with serious music on the basis of the simplicity of the first and the complexity of the second, since the works of harpsichordists or early Viennese classicism are, from a rhythmic and occasionally melodic point of view, less complex than some jazz arrangements. The main difference refers to the dialectic between standardization and non-standardization or, in other words, between reification and non-reification. The repetitiveness, banality and standardization of pop music products is linked to a mechanism of "freezing", socially imposed by industrial cartels, which must propose music that can simultaneously satisfy two questions: (1) the demand for stimuli that awaken the attention of the listener; (2) the demand

---

26 Paddison 1982, p. 208.
27 Adorno 2002c, p. 438.
28 Adorno 2002c, p. 439.

for "natural" music, that is to say, the sum of all the conventions and musical formulas to which he is accustomed and which he considers the intrinsic, elementary language of the music itself[29]. This creates a vicious circle of demand for something that oscillates between new but at the same time familiar and the supply of standardized material covered with familiar novelty. This is the dualistic character of standardization, to which the *pseudo-individualization* is connected, as its necessary correlatum, a mechanism through which mass cultural production is offered cloaked in the aura of free choice or the open market.

In addition to strictly musical issues, there are also considerations regarding the way in which the structure of pop music material is imposed. How does popular music become popular? Thanks to *plugging*, which is a paradoxical "popularization" mechanism for which the publisher wants a song that is at the same time the same and different from other successful pieces, maintaining a certain seductive character, basically melodic, with a certain roundness of sound. The dynamics of plugging are then extended to the personality of the band leaders and listeners. Standardization also concerns the reactions of the listeners.

Pop music, says Adorno, stimulates and consolidates mass listening habits that gravitate around processes of "recognition, identification and ownership"[30]. Adorno proceeds to identify the components that seem to be involved in the recognition process: (a) vague remembrance; (b) affective identification; (c) classification through some label; (d) self-reflection on the act of recognition; (e) psychological transfer of the recognized authority (recognition-authority) to the object. Processes of this nature, together with the characteristics of pop music, can be better understood by paying attention to the "mental scheme" to which that music was originally directed. Popular music takes away spontaneity from the listener and promotes conditioned reflexes, not only depriving him of the effort to follow his concrete flow, but also offering him the same models to which to bring back the concrete that remains. This is made possible and strengthened because the mental scheme to which popular

---

29 Adorno 2002c, p. 444.
30 Adorno 2002c, p. 453.

music is addressed is both "distraction" and "inattention"[31]. After having discussed it in his 1938 essay, In "On Popular Music" Adorno also identified distracted perception as the most widespread way of listening to music. The notion of distraction, central also in Walter Benjamin's analyses (1936), is connected to the modes of production, to the rationalized and mechanized process of work, to which the masses, more or less directly, are subjected. With respect to the rhythms of work, pop music presents itself as a moment of entertainment that fills so-called free time, apparently escaping the mechanisms of production. In truth, it is an illusory parenthesis, a false escape, since it is a situation also determined by the system and mechanisms of production. Popular music ends up becoming a sort of "social cement" that institutionalizes the desires of the masses, like a non-autonomous language (whereas music should be an autonomous language) that everyone thinks they possess but whose deep nature escapes most. Anyone who tries to avoid the consumption of what the agencies propose to millions of people is rejected. An attitude of rebellion is not understood, because "resistance is regarded as the mark of bad citizenship, as inability to have fun, as highbrow insincerity, for what normal person can set himself against such normal music?"[32].

5. Long Live Pop Music

Adorno's critique of popular music has met with many objections, although at the same time it has raised issues that, in some respects, maintain a certain degree of topicality (the mechanisms of "popularization", the repetitive tendencies of commercial popular music, the absence of critical potential). In the corpus of Adornian philosophy, the "critique of popular music is generally considered the least convincing aspect of his otherwise impressive analysis of the predicament of Western music in the twentieth century. The immediate reasons as to why his views on popular music are difficult to accept are obvious enough, and

---

31 Adorno 2002c, p. 458.
32 Adorno 2002c, p. 464.

it must be admitted that the usual criticisms – that Adorno is prejudiced, arrogant and uninformed in this field – contain more than a grain of truth"[33].

While taking these premises into account, Adorno's analysis is weak in several respects. According to Middleton, Adorno highlighted real problems, but exaggerated in homogenizing all the components of the cultural industry and underestimated the tensions and conflicts that characterized some strands of twentieth-century pop music[34]. Adorno has generalized and simplified some mechanisms, reducing the dynamics of listening and receiving to logic of profit and submission, stiffening in an almost incorrigible way the plot of the system of the cultural industry. Moreover, Adorno contrasted two ways of conceiving and practicing music (serious music and popular music), not taking into consideration intermediate possibilities, but this is also because, at the time when he was dealing with popular music, such possibilities were not as numerous as they have been since the late sixties.

Paddison, however, notes how it is possible to produce "an attempt to rescue the baby from the bath water, so to speak, as it seems to me that hidden in his theory there remains a potential which was never properly recognized by Adorno", starting from two basic premises: (1) Adorno's criticism of popular music must necessarily be understood in relation to his analysis of the situation of serious music of the twentieth century; (2) there is no need to expect either positive solutions or simple answers.

The absence of that "differentiating" character typical of Adorno's methodology has certainly hindered the general acceptance of his ideas on popular music. However, according to Paddison, these undeniable defects "should not blind us to the potential contained in the theory as a whole – his negative dialectics – to transcend the personal 'blind spots' which are apparent in his application of the theory to the particular case of so-called popular music"[35]. Paddison then suggests turning to the writings of Adorno on serious music, recovering some theses and applying them to popular music. This could be possible by trying

---

33   Paddison 1982, p. 201.
34   Middleton 1990.
35   Paddison 1982, p. 212.

to translate into pop music what Adorno had identified in serious music, that is, the possibility that he had recognized that some composers, such as Mahler, manipulate tonal and formal material regressed, to the point of making it "authentic". But couldn't the process by which an obsolete or pedestrian material (as Adorno will say about Mahler) be presented in a sublime way also operate in the opposite direction? What Sandner called "pressure"[36] that would push some artists from sub-culture to high culture, "can be understood as being symptomatic of the increasing degree of self-reflection within certain kinds of more radical popular music"[37].

The most radical pop music of the 1960s and 1970s has proved to be fully aware of its function and the nature of its musical material. Using the categories that Adorno applies to serious music, we can say that it undoubtedly had a critical character, not only at the textual level, but also at the constructive and structural level. But, as Paddison writes, "the main point being made here is that a marked feature of certain kinds of jazz and – in particular – rock music since the 1960s is the demand to be taken seriously, the compulsion towards the condition of the serious avant-garde, manifested in the degree of self-examination going on within the music itself. This is a state of affairs which inevitably carries with it its own in-built conflict – its own 'immanent contradiction', as Adorno would have put it"[38].

An example of this is Frank Zappa, among others. As well as reflecting contemporary American reality his music manages to become critical and he does so with imagination, intelligence and irony, yet always with the awareness of having an extraordinary variety of materials and techniques at his disposal. Compared to the coincidence that Adorno proposes between popular music and consumer music, Zappa has shown how musical experience can still provide pleasure and that commitment and entertainment, that engagement and entertainment can coexist, managing to escape the tight links of the system of the cultural industry. Throughout his life, Zappa had a conflictual relationship with the world of music and with the laws of the market, claiming the

---

36 Sandner 1979, p. 130.
37 Paddison 1982, p. 215.
38 Paddison 1982, p. 215.

autonomy and independence of his creations. Just consider the countless proceedings against Metro Goldwyn Mayer and Warner. Consequently, Adorno's critics of popular music find in Zappa a sound refusal.

In an apparently paradoxical way, to really penetrate the music of an artist like Zappa, it would be much more useful to take some pages of Adorno's work dedicated to serious music than those on popular music. As far as the relationship with society is concerned, for example, Zappa's position was a clear contrast to the status quo, trying to expose the contradictions of late capitalist American society. As for the strictly musical aspects, Zappa composed his rock works with the rigor of serious music, working creatively, with an anti-traditional approach. From a harmonic point of view, Zappa's music demonstrates extreme mobility and variability, freeing itself from the most typical solutions of traditional harmony, such as the dominant-tonic cadence, unhinging the procedures and tonal harmonic functions[39].

As Stefano Marino writes, from Zappa's texts and music seems to emerge "a vision of art as a critical voice on society which, faced with the harshness and ruthlessness of the latter, must prohibit the temptation to decorate or embellish reality – which would compromise it on an ideological level and make it useless, or worse, false – and must rather give us back, with its own expressive means, reality itself in all its problematic and contradictory nature. A vision of art, the latter, which – as it is said here *en passant* – seems to present many reasons for affinity with that of Adorno"[40].

We can add one more element. Proceeding with an analogy, which is rather risky, we could say that, in relation to music, we could compare the Adornian dialectic of freedom/commodification to Deleuzean territorialization/deterritorialization. From this point of view, the standardization and repetitiveness of which Adorno speaks would be matched by the notion, in Deleuze, of territorialization. In this perspective, the refrain presents itself as a "territorial articulation"[41], a strategy of definition and appropriation of a space-time. The developments of Western music could be fully

---

39 Montecchi 2017.
40 Marino 2014, p. 74.
41 Deleuze and Guattari 1987.

read in the light of the dialectic between territorialization and deterritorialization, with a tendency, in the twentieth century, for the latter to overtake the former, at least in generic experimental music (which is obviously not only of the so-called "classical" type).

Genres, at their original stage, such as jazz, pop and rock, reveal a high degree of territorialization. Jazz, for example, plays on the relationship between background and foreground, between melody, rhythm and harmony, within schemes which remain substantially always the same. But it is precisely within jazz that the need emerges to overcome this model, to challenge it. This happens with the emergence of free jazz, in the 1960s, which presents itself as an attempt to break away from the standard connections and dismantle the established hierarchies of jazz. An analogous process of taking a distance from a traditional, compacted and "commercial" dimension is found in the field of rock music, which starts from a stage of rigidity analogous to that of original jazz. Rock is organized on the basis of a standard instrumentation that provides a hierarchy that goes from the top to the bottom: voice, lead guitar, rhythm guitar, bass, drums. Nothing could be more conventional. However, as with jazz, the history of rock also includes anti-traditional counter-currents (for example, Velvet Underground or Kraftwerk). During the 1990s, these trends spread and strengthened, because of the pressure exerted by disco music, far from the individualism, masculinity and cult of the personality typical of rock. At that time, rock had basically four possibilities: (a) to take refuge in the cradle of traditional pop; (b) to contaminate itself with different styles and genres, giving life to "hybrid" forms such as psychedelic rock, blues rock, garage, etc.; (c) to choose the way of ideological extremization with punk, heavy metal, etc.; (d) to try to overcome traditional rock, by keeping the standard instrumental ensemble, working on music, which means on its basic constructive elements (melody, harmony, rhythm). In these ways, rock has taken the path of deterritorialization. A similar path has been taken by pop music, especially "liminar" music, which is located in an area very close (or contiguous) to rock, and which is characterized by being authentically "experimental".

Adorno would have argued, using Deleuzean terms, that rock and pop coincide with what is territorial, territorializing or reterritorializing. On the contrary, dodecaphonic music would be at the starting point of a decidedly deterritorialized music era. In fact, Arnold Schönberg is credited with the first profound deterritorialization of classical opera, annulling the "tyranny" of tonality, de-naturalizing the traditional melodic, harmonic and tonal system. Distributed along the entire chromatic scale, atonal music acquired a fluid character and escaped resolution. Nevertheless, there would soon be a re-territorialization, when the unifying principle of tonality would be replaced by that of the series. It was the experimental developments of post-Webernian music, starting in the 1940s, that offered new possibilities for deterritorialization, through the research of Edgar Varèse, Morton Feldman, John Cage, Karlheinz Stockhausen and the generation of composers of electronic, acousmatic and digital music. In this season of twentieth century music, we therefore find the evident traces of all that modern experimentation oriented towards the exploration of the new, the unprecedented, the unheard of.

In this regard, Jean-Jacque Nattiez has effectively pointed out how the "modern" has tried to combine confidence in musical progress with a bold idea: that the experimental music of today would become the universal music of tomorrow. Added to this is the desire to imagine musical progress as something whose trajectory would be parallel to political progress, oriented towards a universal and classless society. Moreover, the modern is in search of purity; Nattiez is convinced of the aesthetic value of his achievements, and has full confidence in the truth of his compositional work. On the other hand, postmodernism has no confidence in the future, according to Nattiez, so it creates works for today's listener, privileges pleasure and does not fear the impurity produced by the mixture of different styles and genres. Moreover, postmodernism tends to consider cultures expressed in different eras as equivalent, since musical creations meet the taste of listeners. Consequently, "there is no longer any a priori barrier or censorship that prohibits recourse to this or that style, this or that writing. The return to tonality is welcome, because it allows the conjunction of so-called serious music with pop and industrial music"[42].

It is therefore interesting to note that in the second half of the twentieth century there was an unusual and almost curious

---

42   Nattiez 2006, p. XXII.

situation, in which radical music, committed to recovering (or creating *ex novo*) a relationship with the public, became almost popular, and popular music, especially rock, tended to become more and more radical. But the question is this: for how long can music maintain a position of balance within the tension between the two opposites? And is it therefore able to resist for a long time without falling into the "popular" category or the "radical" one? "The difficulty lies not only in the music itself; it lies even more in the demands made upon the music by the culture industry. Ultimately decisive is not whatever aims the music itself might have, but rather the way in which the music is consumed in spite of those aims. For, although the possibility of critical self-reflection within popular music indicates that it might be able, perhaps, to neutralize at least some of the effects of the culture industry (depending as these do on the manipulation and mystification of the relations between the production, reproduction and reception of music), there are few signs to show that this has actually been achieved to any lasting extent"[43].

In fact, Paddison notes that marketing and distribution mechanisms have become increasingly complex and effective, but at the same time decidedly constricting, so much as to make it increasingly difficult for any type of music – light, popular or avant-garde, western or non-western – to resist its fate as a commodity. If popular music tries the path of radicality, it inevitably runs the risk of distancing itself from the public, becoming music for the few and therefore can no longer be considered "popular", if not in the limited sense of something that uses elements derived from popular musical material. From this it follows that, for example, some of Adorno's theses can also be applied to certain forms of popular music. By defending serious music, Adorno has formulated theses in this way that, despite himself, have ended up attributing the character of "seriousness" to certain music that he would probably have dismissed. By this I mean that, like serious music, some examples of pop music have reached the most advanced stage of their musical material, have achieved full awareness of the techniques and instruments at their disposal, trying to escape their fate as a commodity.

---

43 Paddison 1982, p. 217.

Bibliography

Adorno Th. W.
1945. "A Social Critique of Radio Music", in "Kanyon Review", vol. VII, n. 2, pp. 208-217.
1953. "Das gegenwärtige Verhältnis von Philosophie und Musik", in E. Castelli (ed.), *Filosofia dell'arte*, in "Archivio di filosofia", pp. 5-30.
1957. "Soziologie und empirische Forschung", in *Soziologische Schriften 1. Gesammelte Schriften*, vol. VIII, Suhrkamp, Frankfurt a.M. 1972.
1959. "Ideen zur Musiksoziologie", in *Klangfiguren. Musikalische Schriften I*, Suhrkamp, Frankfurt a.M.
1963. "Strawinskij. Ein dialektisches Bild" (1962), in *Quasi una fantasia. Musikalische Schriften II*, Suhrkamp, Frankfurt a.M.
1983. "Perennial Fashion – Jazz" (1953), in *Prisms*, trans. by S. and Sh. Weber, The MIT Press, Cambridge (MA), pp. 119-132.
2002a. *Aesthetic Theory* (1970), ed. by G. Adorno and R. Tiedemann, transl. and ed. by R. Hullot-Kentor, Continuum, London-New York.
2002b. "On the Fetish-Character in Music and the Regression of Listening", in *Essays on Music*, trans. by S.H. Gillespie, ed. by R. Leppert, University of California Press, Berkeley, pp. 288-317.
2002c. "On Popular Music" (1941), in *Essays on Music*, trans. by S.H. Gillespie, ed. by R. Leppert, University of California Press, Berkeley, pp. 437-469.
2012. *Introduction to the Sociology of Music* (1962), trans. by E.B. Ashton, Continuum, London-New York.

Arbo A.
1991. *Dialettica della musica. Saggio su Adorno*, Guerini e Associati, Milano.

Benjamin W.
1968. *The Work of Art in the Age of Its Technological Reproducibility* (1936), trans. by H. Zohn, Harcourt, Brace & World, New York.

Bruns G.L.
2008. "On the Conundrum of Form and Material in Adorno's Aesthetic Theory", in "The Journal of Aesthetics and Art Criticism", vol. 66, n. 3, pp. 225-235.

Deleuze G. and Guattari F.
1987. *A Thousand Plateaus. Capitalism and Schizophrenia* (1980), trans. and foreword by B. Massumi, University of Minnesota Press, Minneapolis-London.

Fronzi G.
2011. *Theodor W. Adorno. Pensiero critico e musica*, Mimesis, Milano-Udine.
2016. "Dialettica negativa, metafisica e intersoggettività. Una lettura relazionale del pensiero di Th.W. Adorno", in G. Matteucci and S. Marino (ed.), *Theodor W. Adorno: Truth and Dialectical Experience*, in "Discipline filosofiche", vol. XXVI, n. 2, pp. 187-201.

Hohendhal P.U.
1992. "Adorno Criticism Today", in "New German Critique", n. 56, Special Issue on Theodor W. Adorno (Spring-Summer), pp. 3-15.

Marino S.
2014. *La filosofia di Frank Zappa. Un'interpretazione adorniana*, Mimesis, Milano-Udine.
2018. "Adorno e l'estetica del jazz come *pseudos*", Afterword to Th. W. Adorno, *Variazioni sul jazz. Critica della musica come merce*, Mimesis, Milano-Udine, pp. 115-143.
2019. "Adorno (Against Heidegger) on Style and Literary Form in Philosophy", in "Meta: Research in Hermeneutics, Phenomenology and Practical Philosophy", vol. 11, n. 1, pp. 233-263.

Matteucci G.
2017a. "L'utopia dell'estetico in Adorno", in "Rivoluzioni molecolari", vol. 1, n. 1, pp. 1-9.
2017b. "Adorno's Aesthetic Constellation from Shudder to Fashion. A Form of Life in Age of Globalization?", in "Zeitschrift für Ästhetik und Allgemeine Kunstwissenschaft", vol. 62, n. 1, pp. 41-55.
2018. "Il jazz in Adorno: variazioni in serie", Foreword to Th. W. Adorno, *Variazioni sul jazz. Critica della musica come merce*, Mimesis, Milano-Udine, pp. 7-22.

Middleton R.
1990. *Studying Popular Music*, Open University Press, Buckingham-Philadelphia.

Montecchi G.
2017. *Frank Zappa. Rock come prassi compositiva*, Arcana, Roma.

Nattiez J.-J.
2006. "Come raccontare il XX secolo?", in *Enciclopedia della musica*, III. "Le avanguardie musicali del Novecento", Einaudi, Torino, pp. XV-XLII.

Paddison M.
1982. "The Critique Criticised: Adorno and Popular Music", in "Popular Music", n. 2 ("Theory and Method"), pp. 201-218.
1993. *Adorno's Aesthetics of Music*, Cambridge University Press, Cambridge.

Sandner W.
1979. "Popularmusik als somatisches Stimulans: Adornos Kritik der leichten Musik", in O. Koleritsch (ed.), *Adorno und die Musik*, Universal Edition für Institut für Wertungsforschung, Graz, pp. 125-132.

Serravezza A.
1976. *Musica, filosofia e società in Th. W. Adorno*, Dedalo, Bari.

Stone A.
2016. "Adorno and popular music", in *The Value of Popular Music: An Approach from Post-Kantian Aesthetics*, Palgrave Macmillan, Basingstoke, pp. 69-108.

Zurletti S.
2006. *Il concetto di materiale musicale in Adorno*, il Mulino, Bologna.

Colin J. Campbell
CARRY MY BODY: "PROFANE REDEMPTION" AND FUGAZI

> Precisely those elements of art that cannot be taken immediately in possession and are not reducible to the subject require consciousness and therefore philosophy. It inheres in all aesthetic experience to the extent that it is not barbarically alien to art. Art awaits its own explanation. It is achieved methodically through the confrontation of historical categories and elements of aesthetic theory with artistic experience, which correct one another reciprocally.[1]

The following is an essay in two parts. The first part explores the idea of 'profane redemption' as a notion in critical theory and in popular culture. The second part examines the way an aesthetic theory of redemption which is implicit in the music of Fugazi has been made explicit by Ian Mackaye, with his 2013 address to the Library of Congress. Together, the parts bear out Adorno's notion of 'reciprocal correction' of experience and theory.

1. *Profane Redemption*

this is my last picture

There is a profound ambiguity to Walter Benjamin's notion of *profane illumination*. On the one hand, it points to a radical experience that shatters everyday capitalist consciousness. Surrealism, erupting in the 1910s and 20s, an ecstatic art-movement born from the radioactive energies of technological transformation,

---

[1] Adorno 1997, p. 353.

was making the dream-life real even as capitalism destroyed the traditional expressions of human imagination. In his 1928 essay "Surrealism: the Last Snapshot of the European Intelligentsia", Benjamin wrote that one could receive an "introductory lesson" to "profane illumination" from "hashish, opium or whatever else"[2]. He wrote of the aim of surrealism: "to win the energies of intoxication for the revolution"[3].

But he also acknowledged the heroic period of Surrealism was over. By Guy Debord's time, the spectacle of capital had already absorbed the surrealist tendency. Today, currency itself, as blockchain, has become a privileged object for surreal-immersive *détournement*[4]. How today can we distinguish the tragicomic profane illumination of the body of nature from the ongoing liquidation of the biosphere? Or from the still credible threat of nuclear illumination, which Benjamin could only have imagined? How can the embrace of Aragonian-Rimbaudian evil today transcend Trump's reality show and *House of Cards*? If a world can become such a thin satire of itself, one might marvel at how satire can still be anything other than a morbid affirmation: 'life is beautiful,' 'choose life'[5]. As Guy Picciotto observed at the dawn of this century, "In a room so brightly lit, I can't see in"[6].

In 1928, Benjamin shared the Surrealists' love of the dialectic of the outmoded and the modern city, and he participated in their revolt against French Catholicism and its Republican doubles. But he also said "the religious lesson is stricter"[7]. What does this mean? Whatever its content, it seems to resonate with Benjamin's reason for why Surrealism must necessarily be politicized in a communist direction: "There is always, in such movements, a moment when the original tension of the secret society must either explode in a matter-of-fact, profane struggle for power and domination, or decay as a public demonstration

---

2   Benjamin 1978, p. 179.
3   Benjamin 1978, p. 189.
4   Friend 2017.
5   Benigni 1998; Boyle 1996.
6   Fugazi 2001, from "Oh".
7   Benjamin 1978, p. 179.

and be transformed"[8]. The strict left-politicization of surrealism was the only way, it seemed to Benjamin, to avoid the eternal fate of emancipatory social movements.

But it seems that Benjamin's was a left anti-Catholicism that did not require a rejection of religious lessons. Much theorizing has been brought to bear on the question of Benjamin's irreducibly complex relation to the Judaic tradition. Nevertheless, the problem with pursuing Surrealist profane illumination, as was already becoming the case before Benjamin's eyes, is that today *everything has already been profanely illuminated*. Benjamin knew well that this profaning of all that is holy by way of making everything equivalent was an inherent aspect of capitalist development, yet he located an aspect of heterogeneity contained within the process itself. And it seems that it was the religious lesson that gave the strictest sense of this heterogeneity.

Perhaps we can summarize the complexity of the religious question by saying that Benjamin aimed somehow to shift a blinding profane illumination to the invisible wavelengths of redemption. But "redemption" as a concept can hardly be strictly separated from theology, which in 1940 Benjamin warned must stay out of sight, like a dwarf puppeteer[9]. The puppeteer indeed remains out of sight in Benjamin's "Surrealism" essay – but we do see the strings moving with his remark about the strictness of the religious lesson.

I feel that what Benjamin means is that what brings tone and shape to the otherwise formless mass-illumination provided by commercialism, self-promotion, vapid empty commentary, sexual anomie, and self-evidently worthless hubris to which we are thrown in the spectacle of mechanically reproduced entertainment, is the idea of redemption. Redemption, only redemption, provides the sense of direction, even when our precise location and the distance from the goal remain strictly unknown, or when we appear to be stuck on a one-way street: "The only hope of making sense, all depends on the source of light"[10].

---

8   Benjamin 1978, p. 178.
9   Benjamin 1969, Thesis 1 from *Theses on the Philosophy of History*.
10 Fugazi 1998, from "Closed Captioned".

Is this is why Adorno, in the "Finale" to *Minima Moralia*, wrote that the reality or unreality of redemption matters much less than the possibility of formulating it?[11] In the society of integrated spectacle, the possibility of redemption as an object of theorizing is obscured behind the actuality of totalized profane illumination. It lives, like Adorno's introvert-theorist, on the dark side of a moon taken over by extroverted entertainment technicians.

It must contend with the fact of a commodified, apocalyptic revelation posing as redemption, no longer even quite sure of its capacity to lie, its subject no longer distinguishing mechanical sarcasm from emphatic meaning, lost in a world of communized affect. Any formulation of the possibility of redemption must contend with the conceptual complexity required even to formulate

---

11   Adorno 1974, p. 247.

'redemption,' a word no longer in common use outside of religious fundamentalism and the intellectual élites. The problem is not to know the heart's reasons, but how to measure the gap that exists between them and the everyday 'thinking' that continuously modifies them, for better or worse, always adapting them to the prevailing context.

Critical theory teaches that redemption is hiding in the wings of the surplus-illuminated spot-lit stage of late capitalism. And so, at least since Susan Buck-Morss wrote *Origin of Negative Dialectics*, it has been said by critical theorists (including the present author) that Benjamin and the Frankfurt School have formulated an idea, an ethics and politics of *profane redemption*[12]. I feel it needs to be said that the profane illumination of redemption is a monstrous idea, and not only because 'redemption' is an irredeemably religious word. Rather, "profane redemption" brings to mind both mass-marketed religious fundamentalism and 'retail therapy' – all of what Adorno rightly trashed as "the scum of the culture industry"[13]. Since the 60s, there is less and less any object, sacred or profane, which cannot be 'redeemed for points'. "Profane redemption" itself would first need to be redeemed: "Even its own impossibility it must at least comprehend for the sake of the possible"[14].

shot in real, real realism

Yet Adorno maintained that to publicly formulate redemption in midst of the spectacle can be a radical act. After all, to actually change the world it would be necessary first to rightly interpret it; and we therefore need to be as ruthlessly critical of our own models of redemption as we are of the existing things that deserve to perish. In a continuously innovating world, the impulse to be always *acting* for 'progressive' change can become an obstacle to progress. When human purposes are realized more and more autonomously of their bodies, when activity is perpetual and everywhere, a gesture of passivity before the machine may

---

12 Buck-Morss 1977, p. 89.
13 Adorno and Marcuse 1999, p. 132.
14 Adorno 1974, p. 247.

go beyond a mere bourgeois indulgence. It may actually be an entrée to not only *feeling* the terror and the worthlessness one has felt for a long time, however numbly, and without being able to speak of it – but to be able to put it in such a way as it can be stated publicly.

This terror of worthlessness is the currency of the spectacle. A decrease in the circulation of that currency not only serves the revolution: it is the revolution. Critical theory is saying that to really feel 'it' is the first step to change, however unpleasant the experience may be; but that to *feel* 'it' fully also requires a changed *idea* of objectivity.

But as we shift from objective economic indices to the idea of the idea, we move in that abstract conceptual or spiritual direction that has induced many leftist critics to portray critical theory as bourgeois idealism. In response, we say that the theory of Adorno, Horkheimer, Benjamin, Marcuse *et. al.* does have a distinct spiritual aspect: it is oriented toward a *world which is possible but not materially present*, wherein endemic war, incarceration and criminality, systematic exploitation etc. would be eliminated as factors from human life. This would be no minor welfare reform. It would represent a fundamental alteration of the course of history. Critical theory's vision is *unapologetically messianic*, as its liberal and conservative critics have always argued.

Herbert Marcuse expressed his messianism in psychoanalytic terms – and it is perhaps the absence of explicitly religious language in his corpus that permits Marcuse easier admittance to the private offices of those Marxist purists who have known all along what Adorno and his fellow travelers finally confessed with *Negative Dialectics*[15]. Using Freudian theory in *Eros and Civilization*, Marcuse labeled the ensemble of psychic structures that perpetuate domination as "surplus repression" – i.e. repression in the service of political domination, not part of human nature, but an excessively and gratuitously repressive and violent character imposed on the deeper nature by an historically specific formation. Revolution, as the removal of surplus repression, would unlock

---

15   Adorno 1966, p. XXI. The reason might also be that Marcuse's *Reason and Revolution* is one of the best introductions to Hegel and Marx ever written in English.

unimaginable human potential, shattering the "homogeneous empty time" of wage labour and commodified entertainment. The enemies of change have time and again taken this 'surplus' of repression to be normal, to be human nature, not surplus, and have argued that a change of that nature could only come from God or a god, only from beyond this world. In response, critical theory insists, with and not against the Marxist tradition, "another world is possible"[16].

But the removal of repression does not exhaust or complete the vision of redemption that emerged from Frankfurt. Critical theory cannot avoid an equal and opposite problem: that of accepting basic repression. The Marcusean Freudo-Marxist consciously accepts that some degree of repression, guilt, cruelty, conflict, crime, loneliness, etc. is indelible in human life[17]. So this is no vision of some perfect afterlife or a glorious heavenly revolution of beautiful souls: it is *real*, not in terms of the jargon of authenticity but as a cipher for an unrealized yet pregnant human potential. It would be *real* in the face of necessary loneliness, conflict, loss. It is possible to imagine world without systemic ecological threat, without globalized viral warfare, without needless, highly organized state sponsored acts of brutality. What Rudi Dutschke called 'the long slow march through the institutions' would consist of a plurality of subaltern individuals and organizations producing formulations of redemption for public witnessing and action, whether as art, as science, or as politics in a more direct way. The reality of death does not circumvent the creative spirit of the erotic drive, modulating repetition with change as it does. Utopia has happened before in human history, and *it could happen again* – which is just what Benjamin's dwarf would say, if that subaltern being could only take to the stage and speak openly to us of "profane redemption"[18].

---

16 McNally 2002.
17 For further information, refer to Horowitz 2016.
18 I am referring here to Spivak 1988.

2. The Objectivation of Subjective Experience: Ian Mackaye at the LOC

Ursula LeGuin has observed that 'what science explicates, art implicates'[19]. In this essay I am contending that what critical theory would like to make explicit – this profane redemption that can only be suggested by a theological puppeteer's invisible gestures – is the implicit content and form of the unique and incredible body of work created by Fugazi, a punk rock band from Washington D.C., between 1988 and 2001. In 2013, Ian Mackaye made this connection much more explicit with his address to the Library of Congress.

The fact of resonance between the heights of German inter- and post-war intellectual culture and the noise produced by a bunch of skateboarders (etc.) from Washington still astounds me[20]. I think the music of Mackaye, Picciotto, Lally and Canty distils and purifies something very much like critical theory's idea redemption out of the profane illumination of popular culture. The redemptive aspect of rock and roll has from the beginning been utterly confused with commercialized hedonism – this is the essential tension that defines Fugazi. Their final album, *The Argument*, is not only their swan-song; it plays the last rites for a whole heroic period of American liberalism. Fugazi eloquently prophesied the tragic collapse of the liberal vision of humanity and progress epitomized by John F. Kennedy (in Canada, Pierre E. Trudeau), instantiated by the welfare state, and drawn underwater by the weight of its own internal economic and psychic pathologies.

Fugazi was a local and unique crystallization of the larger punk scene. The band emerged in the mid-1980s, as the ferment of rock and roll and the popular culture as a whole was attaining an unprecedented degree of self-reflection and self-reference. In this sense, punk's relation to Rock resembles that of Euripides to the tragedy of ancient Athens. At one level there is passionate continuity of the direction and movement as a whole: 'tragedy' or 'rock and roll'. But at a deeper level there is a markedly new stage of crisis: Euripides' *Bacchae* is marked by its extreme self-

---

19 LeGuin 2016, from the Foreword.
20 See also my "Three Minute Access: Fugazi's Negative Aesthetic", in Burke et. al. 2007.

referentiality – it is, after all, about Dionysus, the god of theatre, Himself – and also by the extreme moral perplexity into which it cast theatre itself[21]. Nietzsche proposed, in view of this apotheosis of the tragic arts, that in Euripides' hands tragedy died tragically, that it committed suicide[22]. What is the price, poor Agave is left to ask, of the rituals of Dionysus? By the same token, why did Ian Mackaye declare himself 'straightedge'? The context for Fugazi, like that of Euripides, was meta-tragic.

By the time Fugazi released their first album, *13 Songs*, the world was on the cusp of the 'unifying moment' of 1989[23]. Rock and roll had by this time become institutionalized, a normal part of everyday life and commerce for adults as well as youths. Precisely *as* a secret location of spiritual experience, as the image of redemption, it was hooked, lined and sunk into the mechanical heart of the culture industry. Punk was or is a quasi-Euripidean gesture of self-annihilation, raised to the exponent of the music itself. This was music that annihilated self-and-world like Buddhist sand art, exploding in the sky like Jack Kerouac's spiders. The eternal tragic irony is how the very same self-annihilating violence pervades a globe under the perpetual hypnotic commercial suggestion: "always sell, always sell, always sell what we can't own"[24]. While performing their own intense version of the spring rites, Fugazi brought the violence and the lies perennially associated with Dionysianism under interrogation. It might be said that the profound quality of the music lies in the fact of the unreduced tension it maintains between the Dionysian impulse and the ethics of violence. The ambiguity of anger's gift, reduced to a slogan by commercial activist rock, "comes to you, spiritually direct/an attempt, to thoughtfully affect your way of thinking"[25].

---

21   Discussing theatrical self-referentiality in Euripides' *Herakles*, Scott Beauchamp asks "how does a cliché destroy itself?" (Beauchamp 2019). I want to the suggest the question is just as true for *Bacchae*, as well as for punk rock.
22   Nietzsche 1995, p. 36.
23   That the year 1989 became such a spectacularly unifying image-event is the argument of Josh Clover's 2009 text, *1989: Bob Dylan Didn't Have This to Sing About*.
24   Fugazi 1998, from "f/d".
25   Fugazi 1990, from "And the Same".

red-handed

Perhaps Ian Mackaye wanted to tear down that whole great-puppet-show-rock-and-roll-swindle which has only occasionally been interrupted by rattling sounds from beneath the stage[26]. Maybe he wanted to grab hold of the secret promise of rock and roll, which is also the secret promise of critical theory: "the abolition of fear"[27]. In retrospect, following two decades of warmongering and terror, that promise today seems 'sieve-fisted'[28]. But perhaps the public performance of a tragic failure to grasp it is the very essence of Fugazi's collective achievement as musicians.

To say, following LeGuin's dictum, that the critical content of Fugazi's music is implicit might seem odd to those who know the band well, given their overt political and social themes. But it seems to me that they knew their situation too well to let their 'vision statements' ("you are not what you own", "keep your eyes open", "I'm on a mission to never agree", etc.) get in the way of themselves – i.e., to become unqualified, fixed ideologico-political monoliths. In this, they have remained true to what they had promised from the beginning, when Mackaye sang, "we speak the way we breathe"[29]. All their political utterances are woven into the deeper fabric of their origin and destiny – four humans who happen to have found themselves in a popular rock band, near the middle-regions of a commercially-dominated global scene, in America's capital. The music is not and cannot be primarily an opinion or call to action, though those aspects are in the mix. It's most of all a call to *experience* – to experience the experience of the drug-addict, the eccentric weirdo, the public masturbator of the 'Happy Jack' archetype, the anorexic, the shut-in television viewer, the rape victim. The political statements they have made are nothing without their context.

There are doubtless some very worthy social-democratic slogans to be found not only in Fugazi's lyrics but in the vast assembled archive of their live recordings, in conversation with

---

26 Temple 1980.
27 Jameson (ed.) 1977, p. 125 (Adorno writing to Benjamin).
28 Fugazi 1990, from "Sieve-fisted Find".
29 Fugazi 1989, from "Promises".

the audience, interviews, etc. These might ally Fugazi to critical theory superficially, without showing any deeper resonance. The true kinship lies in the experiential fabric of the music, the willingness to see the world redeemed through the splinter-in-the-eye of profane suffering and to publicly express the fact of this *universal guilt that deludes us.*

stacks

What Critical Theory explicates, Fugazi implicates. But Ian Mackaye's marvelous address at the Library of Congress in 2017 has added a new and explicit dimension to the relation[30]. Mackaye has now supplemented his music and interviews with a more or less *explicit theory of mediation* – he has raised the meaning of his public statements in songwriting and elsewhere to the reflective intensity and explicitness of the concept. In *Aesthetic Theory*, Adorno summarized the issue in relation to what Mackaye was talking about: "The totally objectivated artwork would congeal into a mere thing, whereas if it altogether evaded objectivation it would regress to an impotently powerless subjective impulse and flounder in the empirical world"[31].

In his address, Mackaye, like Adorno, draws on his sense of the music itself to produce a set of verbal models. Albeit in a rougher American-English narrative, perhaps a bit more Twain than Goethe, Mackaye nevertheless weaves a *theory* of the relation between recorded music (the 'objectivated artwork') and live experience. He concludes that, while performance and recording lie at opposite poles, what counts is their dynamic relation – and that it is this living, dynamic relation between object and subject, between the frozen image of the past and the dynamic presence-ing of time, of simultaneous repetition and change, that defines or defined the essence of punk[32]. Damage to that paradoxical but

---

30 Mackaye 2013.
31 Adorno 1997, p. 175.
32 I will refrain from weighing in on the by-now archaic twentieth-century question, "is punk dead"? However, it is worth noting that the upshot of Nietzsche's (1995) argument is that Attic tragedy was not so much ended by Euripides as it was institutionalized and Hellenized in the meager form of the New Comedy.

precious relation cannot help but damage the music, as well as its listeners. In other words, Mackaye provides an idea by which to explain the regression of musical taste, its greater and greater fetish character under commercial pressure.

I see them spinning on, so I spin out

Mackaye's talk begins with a characteristic 'anti-flourish': *in media res*, standing here in this Library of Congress, marveling, little punk that he is, at the scale of not only the library itself but of the Internet as a kind of outgrowth or pseudopod of the material place, and at the corollary challenge of documentation in an age of mega-information. In other words, he begins with the kind of gesture of which Fugazi were consistently masterful performers: simultaneously starkly and personally grounded in the present moment, and yet invoking in the moment something much more abstract and general. We might even risk saying – something spiritual. Whatever we call it, it involves a resonating reciprocal interplay between the immediacy of the moment itself and deep historical, political and social experiences.

But the next topic of Mackaye's examination, the matter of documentation, the whole point of Mackaye addressing the Library of Congress, brings a tragic twist, and a warning. He reports that it was precisely the overload and fetishization of commodified musical documentation in the 1970s that had co-opted and undercut the first wave of rock and roll rebellion, that had made punk seem necessary in the first place. The capacity to document, in other words, seemed to have been inseparably fused with the process of commodification. How to break the hold of commodified forms of documentation? How to do so now, in the wake of punk's global commercial success, from the heart of the (post)-imperial Archive?

Mackaye narrates the escape as it began – on a skateboard. Skateboarding was not a weekender's recreation for Mackaye, it was a committed aesthetic act (and so perhaps we might gently modify Adorno's strict lesson, "Every work of art is an uncommitted crime"[33], to allow for minor by-law infractions). Skateboarding,

---

33 Adorno 1974, p. 111.

above and beyond being rebellion against authority, allowed Mackaye and his friends to experience the world in a new way, to see it from a new angle. So – a new beginning, a metaphorical street-level ride out of the state of normal, generalized worthlessness that the commodified world projects on its human inhabitants.

Spinning out, Mackaye falls backward in time, deeper into both autobiography and history. We learn, among other family secrets, that Mackaye's mother's family name was Disney. The irony is sustained as we learn that his mother had worked for some time on a kind of therapeutic-writing-self-help-column practice gone awry. We imagine the culture industry's version of the story, with a soundtrack of Van-Halen-esque guitar crescendo: 'Punking the Library of Congress: Ian Mackaye, Disney's less fortunate son, underdog of the entertainment business, takes vengeance on the Establishment and rocks the Library of Congress!' Well-justified rumours of Mackaye's not inconsiderable personal wealth bring the story perilously close to Horatio Alger.

But see: Mackaye disavows any kind of heroic myth. He only says nonchalantly, those were 'other Disneys'. The crowd laughs warmly. Perhaps it is because they notice how Mackaye is not only evoking but also simultaneously questioning the self-narrative of the 'underdog-become hero'. Do they catch the bottomless sense of irony and humour that seems to coincide with Mackaye's serious, intense demeanor? Perhaps Mackaye would not be satisfied with the recognition given to the underdog who graduates to being the 'Foreman's dog', a new boss for the old boss. Could we go so far as to wonder whether Mackaye might even agree with Adorno's chilly dictum: "glorification of the splendid underdog glorifies the society that makes him so"?[34]

At any rate, it turns out the important point is nothing about Disney. It is that Mackaye's mother's practice, as a therapist, of recording her conversations with her clients on magnetic tape, had spun out into other parts of family life. Snippets of everyday family life were constantly being documented and could then be reflected on. Mackaye narrates his rediscovery of these childhood experiences of living in a family with a mother-as-therapeutic-archivist. And he says that it is from this relation to his mother's

---

34 Adorno 1974, p. 28.

work that was or is born his own alternative to commodified forms of documentation of experience. Is it beyond credibility, at this point, to point to Adorno's "utopia which once drew sustenance from motherly love"?[35]

ejected

Mackaye then flips to another metaphor. Like a spelunker, he says, he went into the underground darkness of punk because the official archive had been so totally commodified, over-illuminated. Music had and has been 'bottled,' and the record player with its vinyl record, the CD player, or the mp3 player – all of which are 'furniture' or appliances – become as indistinguishable from the music as the iconic glass bottle or aluminum can is from the Coca-Cola brand[36]. 'Bottled' music, the Adornian critique might add, reverberates through the sound system as a constant, spiritually deadening imposition of recorded sound on the experience of the listener. We adapt, as Fugazi's metaphor suggests, by learning to understand melody as furniture, embedded as we are in networks of para-musical appliances (ringers, notifications, and above all advertisements emerging from our mobile devices), while mass-digital distribution of apparently 'real' music becomes ever more homogeneous and openly conformist, both technically and thematically[37].

Of course, for humans there must always be interference of records of the past in the present moment, just as there can be no subjectivity without objectivity. This necessity can be related again to Marcuse's concept of basic repression. The sense of rhythm in itself, dimly present in other animals, speaks to some elemental tension in human consciousness, and is surely connected to

---

35   Adorno 1974, p. 23.
36   In describing music in terms of 'furniture' Mackaye is invoking Fugazi's 2001 EP, *Furniture*.
37   Damon Krukowski, formerly the drummer in the American rock band Galaxie 500, explores some overlooked technical and experiential drawbacks of the digital reproduction of sound in *The New Analog* (2017). He is particularly attentive to how the elimination of noise in the signal chain leads to ever more reduced quality of sound in popular music, rather than vice versa. One can only imagine Adorno would have appreciated the irony.

our use of verbal language and our construction of culture. But Mackaye is clearly specifying in his address the *surplus* repressive interference, the willful imposition of 'bottled' music, taking the form lyrically speaking of the *social and psychic predominance of the congealed narrative arc*, the story fragment, the song that is already a logo, a brand.

Through creative arrangement and re-arrangement of broken fragments of concert stories, urban legends and other legends of the overcrowded underground, Mackaye's submission to the Library of Congress has torn up the blueprints of commodified punk narratives. Why, Mackaye asks tragicomically, does the narrative arc of punk so often leave out the credit due to Ronald Reagan? And what to make of Mackaye's scurrilous story of the Indian curse, so reminiscent of the "Smallpox Champion"?[38]

Of course, we already know: 'Punk was (one hundred thousand academics write in unison with PBS) about *confrontation*'! And 'confrontation' merely needs to find a more cheerful, sexier synonym for itself (such as 'disruption') to become a highly exploitable commodity and posture of power. Meanwhile, the expansion of experience-documentation, of which the punk scene was one early sign, has long since degenerated into a reality television show of the kind that presently presides over the White House. Life-documentation-exhibition is now not only the core of the entertainment business, it is quickly assuming a major role as 'experiential education' and 'media literacy' in a school system ever-more oriented, ever-more myopically, to labour-markets.

Mackaye perceives the tensions of the scene, characteristically, with pessimism of the mind. Optimism of the will need not be non-contradictory, of course. His optimistic invocation of a "music" that "can't be stopped", seems to run up against his resolute sense of the forces of commodification in the digital music platforms. The sheer quantity of easily available recorded sound always threatens to render trivial not only what is recorded, but live experience itself. The problem, he explains, is how to construct a "new idea" when, by definition, there is never an audience for a *new* idea, when so many old, broken stories seem permanently fused into a petrified landscape.

---

38 Fugazi 1993, from "Smallpox Champion".

Mackaye promises no fixed or final solution to this quandary, which might be said to be the very substance of critical theory's practical concern as well. The immediate problem is not so much how to plan or to organize, but how to hear without fear the sour notes of the administered society, which metaphorical and real Nazi television hosts are always too happy to send for re-tuning[39]. In Fugazi's music we have found, in broken-reassembled fragments of sound, precisely what Benjamin discovered in hashish: "she now throws us, without hoping or expecting anything, in ample handfuls to existence."[40] "Here it comes"[41].

Bibliography

Adorno Th. W.
1966. *Negative Dialectics*, Continuum, New York.
1974. *Minima Moralia*, Verso Press, London.
1997. *Aesthetic Theory*, University of Minnesota Press, Minneapolis.

Adorno Th. W. and Marcuse H.
1999. "Correspondence on the German Student Movement", in "New Left Review", 233, Jan/Feb 1999, pp. 123-136.

Benigni R.
1998. *Life is Beautiful*, Melampo Cinematographia & Cecchi Gori Group.

Benjamin W.
1969. *Illuminations*, Schocken Books, New York.
1978. *Reflections*, Schocken Books, New York.

Beauchamp S.
2019. "Beyond the Cleft Chin: the Tragedy of Herakles" (available at: https://www.theamericanconservative.com/articles/beyond-the-cleft-chin-the-tragedy-of-herakles; last accessed: July 14, 2019).

---

[39] See for example: https://www.youtube.com/watch?v=bEYfl-X2Jcc, at the 1:05 mark.
[40] Benjamin 1978, p. 145.
[41] Fugazi 2001a, from "The Argument".

Boyle D.
1996. *Trainspotting*, Channel Four Films, Figment Films & The Noel Gay Motion Picture Company.

Buck-Morss S.
1977. *The Origin of Negative Dialectics*, The Free Press, New York.

Burke D. et al. (ed.)
2007. *Adorno and the Need in Thinking: New Critical Essays*, University of Toronto Press, Toronto.

Clover J.
2009. *1989: Bob Dylan Didn't Have This to Sing About*, University of California Press, Oakland.

Friend S.
2017. *Clickmine*. Game/art installation exhibited at NEon Digital Arts Festival, Dundee, Scotland.

Fugazi.
1989. *13 Songs*, Dischord Records, Washington D.C.
1990. *Repeater*, Dischord Records, Washington D.C.
1993. *In on the Kill Taker*, Dischord Records, Washington D.C.
1998. *End Hits*, Dischord Records, Washington D.C.
2001a. *The Argument*, Dischord Records, Washington D.C.
2001b. *Furniture*, Dischord Records, Washington D.C.

Horowitz G.
2016. "Springing the Trap of Repression from the Inside", from *C-Theory* (available at: http://ctheory.net/ctheory_wp/springing-the-trap-of-repression-from-the-inside-lacans-marcuse; last accessed: July 14, 2019).

Jameson F. (ed.)
1977. *Aesthetics and Politics*, Verso Books, London.

Krukowski D.
2017. *The New Analog*, The New Press, New York.

LeGuin U.
2016. *Late in the Day*, PM Press, Oakland.

Mackaye I.
2013. "Special Event: Ian Mackaye. Presentation to the Library of Congress" (available at: https://www.youtube.com/watch?v=AvqtY_7Q7hI&; last accessed: July 14, 2019 from the Library of Congress Youtube channel).

Marcuse H.
1960. *Reason and Revolution*, Beacon Press, Boston.

McNally D.
2002. *Another World is Possible: Globalization and Anti-Capitalism*, ARP books, Winnipeg.

Nietzsche F.
1995. *The Birth of Tragedy*, The Modern Library (Dover Thrift Editions), New York.

Spivak G.
1988. "Can the Subaltern Speak?", in C. Nelson and L. Grossberg (ed.), *Marxism and the Interpretation of Culture*, Macmillan, London.

Temple J.
1980. *The Great Rock and Roll Swindle*, Boyd's Company et. al.

Marco Maurizi

THE UNBEARABLE LIGHTNESS OF MUSIC?
Adorno's Critique of the Music Industry

One of the most enduring clichés about Adorno's philosophy of music is that he didn't appreciate "light music" because of its "lightness". Since music played a key role in his thinking, it is easy to believe that only "serious" music deserves to be enjoyed, and that "light" music is nothing but cultural garbage that should have not even be produced in the first place. While there is a conspicuous number of famous pages in his work that could be gathered to demonstrate such thesis, I think this is the exact antithesis of Adorno's thought. One could even suggest that the real problem for Adorno was not the "lightness" of popular art, but its alleged seriousness. Adorno appreciated the anarchic exuberance of the Marx Bros and Chaplin, for instance. Accordingly, he never criticizes the idea of a "pure amusement"[1], rather the impossibility of such emancipation of aesthetic pleasure within current social conditions. Today we should definitively leave behind the idea that Adorno's theory of popular music derived from a sort of "cultural shock" as an European emigrant[2], not to mention the idea that he somewhat 'despised' American culture and music[3].

Adorno's attack on pop music should instead be understood in the broader context of his criticism of the "culture industry"[4]. Adorno and Horkheimer coined this concept with a specific polemical intent: they wanted to unmask the illusory character of the expression 'mass culture' since the latter seems to imply the democratic, bottom-up nature of mass cultural products. The

---

1 GS 3, p. 164 (Adorno and Horkheimer 2002, p. 114).
2 Santoro 2012.
3 For a rebuttal of such belief, see Janemann 2004.
4 See Witkin 1998; Buhler 2005.

scheme of the culture industry, on the contrary, is what Adorno and Horkheimer call "false identity"[5] between the instance which produces such culture and the public. The culture industry generates a malign circularity between supply and demand, between production and need: the standardization of products and the use of *clichés* are explained as pure technical means, as the necessary consequence of certain productive requirements; at the same time, though, these means create an audience in their image and likeness, and it is with an appeal to the "taste" of such audience that the existence of fashion, subcultures, repetition and even stupidity is justified.

> Interested parties like to explain the culture industry in technological terms. Its millions of participants, they argue, demand reproduction processes which inevitably lead to the use of standard products to meet the same needs at countless locations. [...] The standardized forms, it is claimed, were originally derived from the needs of the consumers: that is why they are accepted with so little resistance. In reality a cycle of manipulation and retroactive need is unifying the system ever more tightly. [...] The mentality of the public, which allegedly and actually favors the system of the culture industry, is a pan of the system, not an excuse for it.[6]

It is not "because of the supposed 'stultification' of the masses", writes Adorno, that "mass culture proves so irresistible"[7]. On the contrary, it is its very omnipresence which transforms it into a social control mechanism[8]. The key concepts here are derived from Marx and Kant: "fetishism" and "autonomy".

First of all, it is important to emphasize that the circularity between supply and demand is not only functional to the production of cheap music. It also produces negative effects on that music which reactionary critics of mass culture consider 'superior' spiritual creations that ought to be safeguarded from barbarism. Adorno was far from such a naive elitism. As Thomson

---

5   GS 3, p. 141 (Adorno and Horkheimer 2002, p. 95).
6   GS 3, pp. 142-143 (Adorno and Horkheimer 2002, 95-96).
7   GS 3, p. 331 (Adorno 2001b, p. 92).
8   GS 14, p. 209 (Adorno 1976, p. 30); GS 3, p. 148 (Adorno and Horkheimer 2002, p. 100).

correctly argues: "Adorno does not subdivide music based on its listeners and explicitly maintains that the difference should not be expressed in terms that imply some form of value: 'highbrow' and 'lowbrow', 'simple and complex', 'naive and sophisticated' [...]. On the contrary, the distinction that Adorno prefers is that between standardized and non-standardized music"[9]. The way in which the cultural industry safeguards the "classics" by elevating them to the rank of masterpieces only confirms their neutralization as mere objects of consumption. Here "a pantheon of bestsellers builds up. The programmes shrink, and [...] the accepted classics themselves undergo a selection that has nothing to do with quality. [...] This selection reproduces itself in a fatal circle: the most familiar is the most successful and is therefore played again and again and made still more familiar"[10]. Anyone, even today, can experience the consequences of such a trend. As Adorno acutely observes, under such circumstances the pleasure caused by listening to a commercial success – regardless of its intrinsic musical content – becomes in principle indistinguishable from the mere fact that we *know* it: "the familiarity of the piece is a surrogate for the quality ascribed to it. To like it is almost the same thing as to recognize it"[11]. Using a Marxian terminology, Adorno draws the conclusion that here the use value of a cultural good is replaced by its exchange value: "the consumer is really worshipping the money that he himself has paid for the ticket to the Toscanini concert. He has literally 'made' the success which he reifies and accepts as an objective criterion, without recognizing himself in it. But he has not 'made' it by liking the concert, but rather by buying the ticket"[12].

The specific quality of a film or a musical piece remains thus external to their diffusion through the media. What matters is the possibility to integrate them into the general mechanism of production: the homogeneity of the culture industry derives in the long run from the fact that each cultural product must fall within pre-established production criteria. Since cultural industry follows the quantitative criterion of success at the box office – i.e. since

---

9   Thomson 2006, p. 47.
10 GS 14, p. 22 (Adorno 2001a, p. 36).
11 GS 14, p. 14 (Adorno 2001a, p. 30).
12 GS 14, p. 24 (Adorno 2001a, p. 38).

its productive drive is always in the end manipulated from above – even qualitative differences in the products ultimately reside in investment, "in the level of conspicuous production"[13]. According to Adorno, the music industry is the opposite of a process of "socialization": "asociality is key to Adorno's radical critique of the culture industry. Its point of departure is Marx's analysis of the fetishism of commodities. [...] In an industrial society which produces goods through an alienated labour process for sale as commodities on a mass market, the products themselves appear, to the individual, estranged from the social relations through which they are produced"[14]. For a real process of socialization to take place, following Marx' analysis of capitalism, a democracy of (intellectual and material) labour should be first established.

This leads us to the problem of "autonomy": as Buhler has shown[15], the "formalist" aspects in Adorno are an attempt to detect the point where art transcends its historical and social conditions. Yet, since Adorno was a materialist, his concept of "autonomy" never means an idealist separation from the sphere of social relations: it indicates the possibility of socialization beyond the current state of things, beyond the realm of dominion and exploitation. Art's promise of social truth should belie the mass deception of culture industry: the dialectical opposition between art and culture industry helps Adorno precisely to articulate the problem of art and socialization without resulting in either elitist idealism, nor in materialist populism[16]. Thus, while "art music" in

---

13 GS 3, p. 145 (Adorno and Horkheimer 2002, p. 97).
14 Witkin 1998, pp. 177-178.
15 Buhler 2005, p. 110 ff.
16 Middleton (1990) attempts a partial 'rehabilitation' of Adorno with respect to the accusations of elitism that are usually addressed to him. In my opinion his defence does not touch the core of Adorno's philosophy and never really questions the hermeneutical stereotypes built around Adorno's figure in the 1970s and 1980s (Middleton, for instance, confuses 'standardization' and 'commercialization', thus totally flattening Adorno's musical and economic model: by doing so, he abolishes the historical-theoretical tension of Adornian musicology replacing the term 'standardization' with the neutral 'formula'). Middleton commits two mistakes: in a certain sense he is *too critical* of Adorno, in another he *doesn't enough criticize* him. On the one hand, in fact, Middleton wants to 'save' popular music from Adorno's attacks without seeing that such criticism is addressed to the cultural industry as a whole and not to

its highest moments resists this process of assimilation – and it does this so well that it has to be "deformed" to fit music industry standards (through the reduction of the value of music to the personal quality of its composer, through the isolation of famous, catchy "melodies" from the body of major and more articulated works, and so on) –, consumer music seems to be nothing but an expression of culture industry's greed for profit. It doesn't need to adapt itself to it. This explains why Adorno often interprets musical hits from a *sociological* point of view, why his analyses of light music never fall within the scope of his *philosophy* of music alongside Mahler, Schönberg or Stravinsky.

The impossibility of a "philosophy of mass music" seems to reside precisely in the preponderance of the productive apparatus over the individual features of the musical object, something which makes light music incommensurable to what Adorno calls "autonomous art". Not only would the single song not exist without such apparatus, but, as we have seen, it must also correspond to general criteria of saleability in order to be produced and distributed. A great part of its "form", thus, has little to do with intrinsic musical values. Since light music is dominated by a general productive scheme, an analysis that aims at immediately grasping its uniqueness and unrepeatability would be possible, but false in the end. When Adorno attempted analysis of consumer music he tried to highlight the musical mechanisms that produced effects of 'dullness' or 'regression' of listening, by comparing the compositive level achieved by "serious" composers to that of radio hits.

---

individual songs, nor to any of their 'intrinsic' musical characteristics; secondly, I believe that it is only by *accepting* Adorno's criticism of popular music that it is possible to understand the musically progressive developments of rock history and, therefore, to recognize the limits of Adorno's theory. Something analogous happens in the history of jazz. Attempts to criticize Adorno's theory of jazz (Schonherr 1991; Gracyk 1992) are usually based on (1) radical developments in jazz composition and improvisation from the 1950s and 1960s (which directly challenged the primacy of swing and tonality attacked by Adorno!), (2) less known repertoire from famous artists of 1930s and 1940s: all this *confirms*, rather than contradict, Adorno's statements on the formal rigidity of traditional jazz and the role played by culture industry in shaping the mass experience of jazz music (Witkin 1998; Buhler 2005).

This regression can be described in terms of "fetishistic listening": the ear is led to listen only to partial elements of the music (a melodic fragment, a particular timbre, the insistence of a rhythmic figuration, etc.), fixing itself to them as fetishes, without being able to unify them, without being able to give them *meaning* within the totality of the composition. While, according to Adorno, the *telos* of serious music (from Bach onwards) was to integrate all the dimensions of the composition into a significant totality, so that the particular only *means* something as a moment in the *development of the whole*, the culture industry aims at the enhancement of the isolated effect and assembles for this purpose a kind of music that leads to *atomized* listening. If art music has produced over the centuries a differentiation of musical details (from the autonomy of the parts to the elasticity of the rhythm, from the amplitude of the dynamics to melodic and harmonic richness etc.) it has always subjected its innovations to the "law of form". On the contrary, in mass music the isolation of single perceptual stimuli is functionless, musically absurd. Here the particular is autonomous only in the sense that it denies the possibility of the universal, it prevents the comprehension of the whole[17].

Yet, this process takes place only because the alleged "tastes" of the public need songs built according to infantile, superficial and unrelated desires. Here the circularity between production and the needs of the masses becomes apparent from a strictly musical point of view. "Pop melodies and lyrics must stick to an unmercifully rigid pattern. [...] Above all, it is the metric and harmonic cornerstones of any pop song, the beginning and the end of its several parts, that must follow the standard schema. It confirms the simplest fundamental structures, whatever deviations may occur in between. Complications remain without consequences"[18].

Such rigidity produces certain mechanical traits of light music, which could easily be written by a machine. What in principle excludes it, is the function that the "human" element still plays in the ideological apparatus of the cultural industry. Such "artisanal" aspect, i.e. something which is never 'fully planned' in the industrial

---

17 GS 14, p. 18 (Adorno 2001a, pp. 32-33).
18 GS 14, pp. 203-204 (Adorno 1976, pp. 25-26).

sense, is always needed and welcome. Industrial music is, so to say, forced to a peculiar kind of Sisyphus' work: it must express the greatest possible proximity to the listener despite the prevailing standardization of its methods. Only the human element can realize the paradoxical formula of the consumer song: "On the one hand it must catch the listener's attention, must differ from other popular songs if it is to sell, to reach the listener at all. On the other hand, it must not go beyond what audiences are used to, lest it repel them. It must remain unobtrusive, must not transcend that musical language which seems natural to the average listener envisaged by the producers-that is to say, the tonality of the Romanticist age, possibly enriched with contingencies of impressionistic or later derivation"[19]. Thus, the commercial successes baked by Tin Pan Alley represent the musical equivalent of mass-produced family houses, and perfectly mirror the constitutive contradiction of the cultural industry: designing and producing the "repetition of the unrepeatable (*Wiederholung des Unwiederholbaren*)"[20].

The fact that the form is imposed "from above" determines the structural "ahistoricity" (*Geschichtslosigkeit*) or timelessness of the song form. Art music, on the other hand, focuses on time and dominates it through the organization of its internal conflicts; only in this way does music realize its own "transcendence" with respect to empirical, real time[21]; the creative power of the composer welcomes time as a moment in the development of music, so time becomes the *medium* of construction, it helps synthesize the parts in the whole. Yet, the properly musical succession is accomplished not *by virtue* of the chronometric time but *against* it. Otherwise it merely parasitizes the temporal flow[22]. Precisely this seems to happen in consumer music, where time is the mobile background on which untied musical events take place, without any structural contrast, without any tension that could bring music to tear and transcend its scheme. "Musical time becomes meaningful as the transition to the nonidentical"[23], the tempo of the song offers only a pale simulacrum of "experience" and establishes, from a

---

19 GS 14, p. 210 (Adorno 1976, p. 31).
20 GS 3, p. 317 (Adorno 2001b, p. 79).
21 GS 3, p. 312; GS 14, p. 152; GS 16, p. 494.
22 GS 16, p. 518.
23 Hullot-Kentor 2006, p. 188.

sociological point of view, the triumph of identity (what Adorno calls *das Immergleiche*, "always-the-same"). The function of pop music, therefore, is to hide "the desolation of the inner sense. It is the decoration of empty time"[24]. In other words, while pop music masks with its bright colors the fact that the administered world makes it impossible to experience something which transcends it, classical music, *maxime* the uncompromising avant-garde, offers the image of a radical, irreducible alterity.

It is important to stress that Adorno's criticism of the music industry never attacks the musical meaning or value of songs pitching them against the complexity of art music. His concern is rather, the fact that they will contribute through their immanent mechanism of repetition to cementing the dependence of the public on the dominant cultural apparatus. Contrary to what Middleton believes[25], Adorno conducted sympathetic analysis of popular hits during his American period and underlined the importance of not confusing the interpretation of classical music with that of popular music, because the material of which the latter is composed implies that, "paradoxical as it seems, the analysis of hits, too, has to be handled in a much subtler and more differentiated way than in most cases of serious music if any concrete result is to be yielded"[26]. Adorno stresses that the problem of light music is *never* its simplicity, since "simple" and "complex" are relative concepts and it would not make sense to judge the organization of the material used in pop music through the forms of classical music. Adorno even notices that in some cases the harmony and rhythm of light music can be even *more complex* than some pieces of classical music.

The problem, therefore, should not be placed at the level of the single song, nor of the simplicity of the compositional procedures: but of the sphere of light music as a *whole* and the way in which industrial production introduces standardization as a practice. It is with respect to these phenomena that Adorno attempted to highlight the mechanisms that produce effects of "dullness" or "regression" of listening in popular music. The mechanism of

---

24 GS 14, p. 228 (Adorno 1976, p. 47).
25 Middleton 1990, p. 34 ff.
26 CM, p. 329.

repetition and the consequent recognition of a musical element constitute in fact the primordial level of listening beyond which the phenomenon of understanding of the musical sense is constituted: this is closely linked to the production of something "new" that is not identified with the mere perception of sensory stimuli. Music is surely made of stimuli, but the meaning of music is evoked by something which happens 'beyond' the sphere of mere sensation.

> The musical sense of any piece of music may indeed be defined as that dimension of the piece which cannot be grasped by recognition alone, by its identification with something one knows. It can be built up only by spontaneously linking the known elements – a reaction as spontaneous by the listener as it was spontaneous by the composer – in order to experience the inherent novelty of the composition. The musical sense is the New – something which cannot be traced back to and subsumed under the configuration of the known, but which springs out of it.[27]

However, this severe judgment also explains why Adorno's criticism of the cultural industry is *not* elitist and aristocratic. The "regression of listening" of which Adorno speaks is not a form of degeneration from a golden age of serious appreciation of music: "This does not mean a relapse of the individual listener into an earlier phase of his own development, nor a decline in the collective general level, since the millions who are reached musically for the first time by today's mass communications cannot be compared with the audience of the past. Rather, it is contemporary listening which has regressed, arrested at the infantile stage"[28].

The childish language of consumer music, according to Adorno, is specifically prepared for this purpose and teaches the hatred against anything that might be different. "The regression is really from this existent possibility, or more concretely, from the possibility of a different and oppositional music"[29]. This is why the apparently irrevocable judgment on pop music coexists in Adorno with a persistent hope for change. While he admitted

---

27   CM, p. 300.
28   GS 14, p. 34 (Adorno 2001a, p. 46).
29   GS 14, p. 34 (Adorno 2001a, p. 47).

that, given the actual overwhelming power of the industry over the individual, there was a sort of perverse agreement between production and public needs, he considered the repeated appeal to the "tastes" of masses an ideological trick: "The controllers need that ideology. The slightest relaxation of their control over minds has today an explosive potential, however distant-a potential that is choked off with the hue and cry of unsaleability"[30]. Since the culture industry needs the appearance of the *brand new* in order to hide the sameness of its underlying schemes, "the bad infinity of this hopeless effort of repetition is the only trace of hope that this repetition might be in vain, that men cannot wholly be grasped after all"[31].

It is my intention to show how this analysis of Adorno was not only altogether correct but how the changes occurred in the culture industry since the 1960s have substantially, albeit paradoxically, confirmed it. In Adorno's theory the culture industry is defined by three factors: (1) it cannot really be the expression of a creative, bottom-up movement; (2) its products are structurally devoted to repetition; (3) it is not possible for this circularity to reach self-awareness and to transcend itself ("Popular music can no more be exploded from within, on its own premises and with its own habituated means, than its own sphere points beyond it"[32]). It is true that forces which act in the opposite direction have always existed in the cultural sphere since the dawn of Modernity, but they are powerless in the face of the overall mechanism of the market: only a radical social revolution could change the structure of the culture industry[33]. For this reason, even rebellion against the scheme, which is part and parcel of the communicative strategy of the culture industry, is always measured in advance, it is always – essentially – pseudo-rebellion, pseudo-activity, "ecstasy without content"[34]: "A hit song is treated more leniently today if it does not respect the thirty-two bars or the compass of the ninth than if it includes even the most elusive melodic or harmonic detail which falls outside

---

30 GS 14, p. 401 (Adorno 1976, pp. 200-201).
31 GS 3, p. 331 (Adorno 2001b, p. 93).
32 GS 14, p. 213 (Adorno 1976, p. 34).
33 ZK, p. 290.
34 GS 14, p. 41 (Adorno 2001a, pp. 52-53).

the idiom. Orson Welles is forgiven all his offences against the usages of the craft because, as calculated rudeness, they confirm the validity of the system all the more zealously"[35].

In consumer music, for example, one always remains in the ambit of tonality and every harmonic novelty is introduced only as long as it is congruent with the general scheme; if it cannot be adequately balanced, it must appear as an isolated extravagance, deprived of any structural consequence. Thus, since the 'foreign' elements that oppose the scheme never get a real chance to negate it, they end up reinforcing it. "It cannot be said that interest in the isolated colour or the isolated sonority awakens a taste for new colours and new sonorities. Rather, the atomistic listeners are the first to denounce such sonorities as 'intellectual' or absolutely dissonant"[36]. Adorno thought that light music constantly borrows the scraps of progress taking place in classical music: it cannot produce its own technical advancement in terms of composition.

> The technical innovations of mass music really don't exist. This goes without saying for harmonic and melodic construction. The real colouristic accomplishment of modern dance music, the approach of the different colours to one another to the extent that one instrument replaces another without a break or one instrument can disguise itself as another, is as familiar to Wagnerian and post-Wagnerian orchestral technique as the mute effect of the brasses. Even in the techniques of syncopation, there is nothing that was not present in rudimentary form in Brahms and outdone by Schoenberg and Stravinsky. The practice of contemporary popular music has not so much developed these techniques as conformistically dulled them.[37]

From a certain point of view, Adorno was contradicted by what happened since the 1960s in the field of rock music: light music revolutionized its language and gave life to an immanent development that is not understandable if one does not analyze it from a technical-compositional point of view. In 1967 The

---

35   GS 3, p. 150 (Adorno and Horkheimer 2002, p. 102).
36   GS 14, pp. 38-39 (Adorno 2001a, p. 50).
37   GS 14, p. 47 (Adorno 2001a, p. 57).

Beatles and Pink Floyd released respectively *Sgt. Pepper's Lonely Heart's Club Band* and *The Piper At The Gates Of Dawn* inaugurating a true musical revolution in pop music. Without going into the origin and the socio-political significance of such change – which is also important[38] – let us limit ourselves to trace its musical prehistory starting from an incidental Adornian observation. In some piano reductions of hit singles from the 1930s, Adorno noted with horror the presence of guitar diagrams that indicated the chords; these "musical traffic signals", as he called them, indicated the harmonic change through "visual directives" with no relation whatsoever to musical logic, or the movement of the voices[39]. What Adorno could not imagine was that a whole generation of musicians who grew up playing those diagrams, totally unaware of harmony and counterpoint, would one day replace the professional arrangers and composers of Tin Pan Alley, demolishing all the false musical scaffolding built during the first half of the century by the culture industry. Disrespectful of the song form, they turned it upside-down, looking for the new, the fresh, the unheard, driven by precisely the kind of need that Adorno thought was impossible in current society. Like barbarians of barbarism, they elevated barbarism to a new quality. This revolution was progressively imposed on the culture industry, by a "bottom-up" movement whose needs these works meet and contributed to spread. Their language was articulated by denying what Adorno considered the iron cage of consumer music: such immanent negation, in a way, practically reflected its theoretical criticism. In "Astronomy Domine" the harmonic movements are quite surprising for a piece of light music. They can only be read as an effective search for unheard solutions starting from a standardized idiom. In "Strange Days" by the Doors the harmonic field of the refrain is clearly defined by a search for the unpredictable chord sequence.

---

[38] See Frith 1978; Friedlander 1996.
[39] GS 14, p. 40 (Adorno 2001a, p. 51).

The ambiguity of these chordal passages, the difficulty of even translating their logic into the nomenclature in use for classical music derives from the tendency among rock musicians of regarding a chord as a being-in-itself, an entity whose existence is independent from any harmonic progression. Chords, in other words, pre-exist their structural function and, in some way, always exceed it: chords are nothing but sound-masses centered on a note (the one that, generally, gives its name to the chord) that can be moved and modified at will. These modifications, which are indicated by what Adorno ironically called "traffic signals" (Dmaj7, Dsus2, D5+ etc.) generally concern the periphery of the chord and never affect its center. In this way one can add them to the chord without implying a movement of the voices: chord changes are simply as a fact of which the listener has to "take note". In a way, every chord actually has a tonic function (assuming that one can still speak of a "tonic") and only locally and temporarily assumes a structural function: like the brutal Bb of "Astronomy Domine" that "resolves" on G – a passage that the ear ends up perceiving as VIb-I – or the fleeting fifth (Bb -F) that dominates in the tortuous refrain of "Strange Days".

Even from a rhythmic point of view the mid-1960s revolution expressed the need to break with what was perceived as a constraint: here too, the introduction of a change of time within a single piece is no longer taken as mere 'variation', but as something interesting in itself. "Happiness Is A Warm Gun" literally disintegrates the structure of the song form, adding an incredible series of different times without any regularity.

Beatles, *Happiness Is A Warm Gun*

[musical notation: A soap im-pression of his wife which he ate and do-na-ted to the Natio-nal Trust / I need a fix 'cause I'm going down down to the bits that I left up-town / I need a fix I'm'cause going down Mother su-per - iorjump the gun / Mother su-per - iorjump the gun Hap-pi-ness]

Finally, it is difficult to talk again about "song" for a piece like "Interstellar Overdrive" by Pink Floyd which, while placing the exposition of the main theme at the beginning and end, was created, performed and recorded in the vein of a total, informal and dissonant improvisation.

In these songs a qualitative leap is clearly perceptible in the history of light music: the passionate search for melodic and harmonic novelties, timbres, rhythms etc. expresses a radical and immanent overthrow of the standard idiom of pop songs. Anyway, we must not forget two things. It is obvious that, isolated from the historical context in which they appeared and from the far more radical developments that they inaugurated, the musical examples we have just proposed may not sound persuasive and the paradigm-shift we have suggested may not appear immediately obvious. Consider, for example, the harmony of "I've Been Loving You Too Long" by Otis Redding which in many ways anticipates certain chord movements of English and American psychedelia. In these passages, however, the generally magniloquent and solemn quality of the music affects the harmonic development, tying the chords to the expressive, romantic needs of the voice. In the examples given, on the contrary, the idea begins to take hold that where the musical results are no longer consistent with the song-form, the latter should be sacrificed in the name of a passionate *recherche* of the unexpected. Secondly: we're talking about records that peaked high positions in the sales charts, which were inspired by formal innovations created outside the official circuits (the music scene that would be soon labeled 'underground') and contributed with their success to amplify and raise such repressed desire for musical change. In fact, these innovations did not in the long run go without structural consequences, as the subsequent history of rock music shows. They pushed towards the abandonment of the song-form and the search for wider and more articulated forms that could coherently convey the new musical material that had being brought to light. All this not without difficulty. Music, freed from the strings of the song-form, started to move as in a void: such auroral experimental period inaugurated the search for a whole, a sort of synthesis had to be established starting from an unstable and imperfect language. The difficulties that musicians soon encountered in shaping these wild and inarticulate sounds, in making them speak in a coherent and persuasive way, were in fact due to an insufficient reflection on the constitutive fragmentation of such language, on the fact that its immediacy was an illusion, since it was a "second nature", a language derived from the rests of the musical tradition. Hence the tendency to reorganize the chaos by resorting to models derived from classical music (such as the suite, the concert, the opera etc.) which, however, turned out to be incongruous with respect to the rigidity of such second-hand musical material.

It is obvious that if Adornian concepts are transformed into static and over-historical categories, his analysis of pop music might sound banal and elitist. If we assume instead that philosophical categories have (like the object they are supposed to comprehend) a historical *dynamic*, we understand how rock music has contradicted *and* confirmed Adorno's analysis. If, from one side, we must underline how rock music represented a moment of openness and change that Adorno's analysis deemed as impossible, from the other we must recognize that its inner drive tried to overcome the structural limits of pop song envisaged by Adorno. We must also never forget that such longing for creative innovation was soon to be integrated and normalized by the culture industry. After a brief period of experimentation, the productive mechanism of the industry took over again, restructuring itself around the dissonances that reflected the new needs of the public, domesticating its disruptive force. The "symphonic rock" of the 1970s (Genesis, ELP, Yes etc.) expressed a need for "order", a sort of "restoration", in line with the "seriousness" and "spiritual" grandeur of the 1930s: rock music had become an "adult" and "respectable" thing. The third and final taboo of the cultural industry could not be overcome without a social change, as Adorno had predicted[40].

Maybe such descendant parable of rock music was the consequence of the historical misunderstanding generated by the convergence between the sphere of art and that of the culture industry: both "pop art" and "rock music" dwelled in an illusory no man's land between art and consumption. *Sgt. Pepper* (whose cover was signed by pop artist Peter Blake; consider also the collaboration between Andy Warhol and The Velvet Underground) expressed both the utopia of a new mass music, as well as the germ of the future involution. The case of "A Day In The Life" is striking: "Because of all this Cage and Stockhausen stuff [...] I thought 'OK. I'd try this idea on John' and I said let's take 15 bars, count 15 bars and we'll do one of these avant-garde ideas. We'll say to all the musicians, 'You've got to start at the lowest note on your instrument, which is like a physical limitation, and go to your highest note'. Normally it's all written down in orchestration. [...] *But the avant-garde thing* was that you can go at any speed you want"[41]. Now, if this experiment still reflects the tendency observed by Adorno according to which light music distorts and normalizes what happens in serious music, it also showed what was happening between the two spheres. Maybe better than the coeval, algid production of autonomous art could do. When we talk about Adorno's critique of consumer music, in fact, we tend to forget the parallel criticism that Adorno moved against the avant-garde: a sign that, under capitalism, serious music certainly wasn't doing better than pop[42]. Didn't the fact that it was possible to neutralize the most terrible dissonance testify of an objective *senescence* of

---

40 See Maurizi 2018.
41 McCartney 1989, p. 52.
42 Hullot-Kentor 2006, p. 169.

modern music, as Adorno himself wrote?[43] The superficial and triumphant approach between autonomous art and mass art (e.g. between pop art and rock music) must therefore be understood as the ideological reflection of a condition of objective decline of the former, of its ability to oppose the world-as-it-is.

At the time, avant-garde music was in a state of stalemate both with respect to its social role and its internal impulse. Reduced to a mere cultural minority asset, administered itself by experts, radical music ended up finding itself in a *continuum* with the cultural industry that threatened to undermine its oppositional force. The social imprisonment of the avant-garde in totally integrated societies affected its musical content, from within the aesthetic and compositional sphere, and was mirrored by the false antithesis between Cage and Stockhausen, "chance" and "serialism". Quoting György Ligeti, Adorno remarked how the opposite ends of total integration and absolute randomness, the complete rationalization of music and the "abandonment of any musical logic", in fact, would touch without any reconciliation[44]. By making "inhumanity" their trademark, both poles constituted the aporetic but consequent outcome of that long-term tendency of classical music aimed at integrating all the elements of the composition into a self-sufficient wholeness that constituted, as we have seen, its *differentia specific* from light music. Postwar radical music brought this search for expressive purity to the paradox of inexpressiveness and "de-subjectivation". By questioning all the components of the musical language that had enabled the formal organization of music (including those admitted by Schönberg and his School), in fact it definitively alienated itself from the subject.

Adorno protested against this process: "It is not expression as such that must be exorcised from music, like an evil demon – otherwise nothing would be left except the design of resounding forms in motion (*die Tapetenmuster tönend bewegter Formen*) – rather the element of transfiguration, the ideological element of expression, has grown threadbare. The ideological element is to be recognized in what fails to become substantial in the musical

---

43   GS 14 pp. 143-167 (Adorno 2002a).
44   GS 14, p. 379 (Adorno 1976, p. 181).

form, what remains ornament and empty gesture. What is needed is for expression to win back the density of experience [...], though without being satisfied with parading the cult of inhumanity under the guise of the cult of humanity"[45].

Radical music, both in its serial and random tendencies, ends up celebrating the present state of society in spite of its urgency for radical alterity. Adorno does not solve the doubt about the social and aesthetic meaning of such steadiness: is radical music putting on paper "a seismogram of reality" or has it definitively been consigned to reification?[46] At any rate, Adorno insists that it was precisely the tension that one can still perceive in the works of Schönberg, Berg and Webern that made them "alien" to the dominant consciousness, i.e. alienated from alienation. "Because the currently created music hardly knows-or at least hardly shows-that tension any longer it is less provocative, no longer something radically other than the listeners' consciousness"[47]. In the face of such paradoxical situation, Adorno published an intervention entitled "Difficulties" asking himself whether composing had not become "an ideological operation" in itself and if one should not draw the conclusion that silence was a better choice than making music[48].

This abyss where radical music is driven by its own uncompromising purity, however, seems to open the field to an intriguing theoretical reversal. If the heroic coherence of classical music leads the composer dangerously close to mutism, light music reminds us of the need to say even in the face of the impossibility of saying. This is why Adorno, paraphrasing Willy Haas, stated that if some "good music" can be "bad", one should not be surprised that some "bad music" can be "good"[49]. The fact that, despite the incessant changes of fashion, some pieces of light music "do not pass" and end up becoming *evergreens*, must be explained, according to Adorno, by some intrinsic quality of music itself, not to manipulation:

---

45 GS 14, p. 156 (Adorno 2002a, p. 191).
46 GS 14, pp. 380-381 (Adorno 1976, p. 180).
47 GS 14, p. 383 (Adorno 1976, p. 184).
48 GS 17, p. 253-291 (Adorno 2002b, pp. 644-680).
49 GS 14, p. 211 (Adorno 1976, p. 32).

We may look for it in the paradoxical feat of scoring, with wholly shopworn and platitudinous material, a musical and perhaps expressive hit on a specific and unmistakable target. In such products the idiom has become a second nature, permitting something like spontaneity, idea, immediacy. In America, the self-evident reification recoils at times, unforced, into a semblance of humanity and proximity-and not just into a semblance.[50]

Here, what Adorno denounced as atomistic and partial, turns dialectically into an unexpected positive quality, a "corrective of the upper art":

Popular music shelters quality that was lost in the higher but had once been essential to it, a quality of the relatively independent, qualitatively different individual element in a totality. It has been pointed out by Ernst Krenek and others that the category of the idea, which is phenomenological rather than psychological, loses some of its dignity in the higher music; and it seems as though the lower unwittingly meant to make up for that. The few really good song hits are an indictment of what artistic music forfeited by making itself its own measure, without being able to make up the loss at will.[51]

Adorno's reflections on the expressive decadence of serial and post-serial music constitute a decisive and, I would add, necessary counterpart to his disqualification of light music, seen as a jumble of stimuli opposed to the integrated totality of classical music. Such "organic" totality is definable only *negatively*, as an "anti-mechanical" ideal: every time a musical rule becomes sterile and empty it turns out to be mechanical[52]. No fixed set of rules, no style, no social position occupied by a work or by a composer can be a guarantee that music does not degenerate and become meaningless or reactionary. These are *historical* determinations which, as such, are subject to historical change: under different circumstances, a certain kind of music can even mean the opposite of what it meant when it was originally composed. The struggle against false immediacy, against cheap expressiveness conducted by avant-

---

50 GS 14, p. 216 (Adorno 1976, p. 36).
51 GS 14, p. 216 (Adorno 1976, p. 36).
52 GS 16, p. 526 (Adorno 1994, p. 307).

garde music in the name of true humanity, unintentionally results in an unexpressive void, in which tension and, in the end, even musical logic is lost. At the same time, the immediacy to which Adorno points in his re-evaluation of light music is precisely what the above-mentioned examples of experimental rock music have fought against. Though the mid-1960s revolution inaugurated a sort of genetic mutation of the musical material, rock music's attack against the fake "naturality" of pop language could never reach full transparency, its development was blocked by its own formal and social contradictions. Although partly freed from the immediacy of consumer music, rock could never really stand up to "autonomous" music and its subsequent integration into the establishment was a consequence of the fact that it still celebrated an illusory emancipated subject, in front of which the moment of truth of the anti-subjectivism of serial and post-serial music preserves its aura of legitimacy. Avant-garde music dissolves the fake subject[53], without being able to positively announce a new one, because in the false state the promise of happiness "can no longer be found except where the mask has been torn from the countenance of false happiness"[54].

However, if the technical and ideological development of rock can still be framed in Adorno's musicology of light music, confirming its premises and conclusions, Frank Zappa undoubtedly pushed rock music to such a level of self-awareness and strict control over its formal procedures that completely blew the opposition between serious music and light music. Zappa starts from the inside of pop music operating a sort of immanent denial of its mechanical constraints. The process of "genetic mutation" of musical language assumes in the Zappa's music and imaginary the traits of what is "monstrous" and "repellent"[55]. For Zappa is

> the scandal of all bourgeois musical aesthetics. They call him uncreative because he suspends their concept of creation itself. Everything with which he occupies himself is already there. He accepts it in its vulgarized form; his themes are expropriated ones.

---

53 GS 16, p. 526 (Adorno 1994, p. 280).
54 GS 14, p. 19 (Adorno 1976, p. 33).
55 See Watson 1996; Maurizi 2001.

Nevertheless, nothing sounds as it was wont to; all things are diverted as if by a magnet. [...] Such music really crystallizes the whole, into which it has incorporated the vulgarized fragments, into something new, yet it takes its material from regressive listening.[56]

Adorno wrote these words to celebrate Gustav Mahler who, moving from a musical language pregnant with historicity, uttered for the last time in the area of serious music a positive word of liberation that subtracted it from the spell of identity, leading it beyond the opposition between upper and lower music. Similarly, Zappa was the event that crept into the cultural industry bringing the dialectic between art and consumption to a new stage, overcoming the stalemate of which Adorno had offered a ruthless diagnosis. His work continually defuses the apparent obviousness and naturalness of musical language, without ever passing into an abstract and empty denial of the human. The irony and relentless satire that his music unleashes leaves no room for doubt about his "humanistic" purpose; Zappa's iconoclasm, his ferocious dissolution of the subject-fetish, are to be understood in terms of liberation from inhumanity. This is why the comparisons with Stravinksy – which Zappa also admired and whose rhythmic complexity he did celebrate in his own scores – remain partial and, in the end, unfair[57]. The distance between the severe but human laughter of Zappa against the *plastic people* and the sadistic grin that explodes in the *Sacre*, perfectly expresses the double nature of the *Lachen* mentioned by Adorno and Horkheimer in the *Dialectic of Enlightenment*[58].

It is important to note that Zappa's satire is never extrinsic to its objects, since it tends to deconstruct them from within. Both the stereotypes of pop music and those of the avant-garde are sabotaged by Zappa, both through a process of self-disintegration and through the principle of assembly. Zappa denounces the fakeness of their self-sufficiency, but not their moment of truth (as Adorno himself would have said: the immediacy of pop music and the autonomy of classical music). Once again, though, if Zappa makes Adorno's pessimism about the cultural industry anachronistic, he confirms

---

56   GS 14, p. 49 (Adorno 2001a, pp. 59-60).
57   Watson 1996, p. 56-61.
58   GS 3, pp. 96-97.

his thesis in the last instance. Pop music and classical music can be understood only as halves of a whole that transcends them: Mahler's promise of a music freed from their antagonism; yet, it must be said, that Zappa's musical utopia – parallel but different from Mahler's – was made possible precisely by the totalitarian horizon of the cultural industry, in which serious music and light music are reduced to administrative districts, i.e. aesthetically neutralized, deprived of their social truth. It is not for mere cynicism that Zappa continually defines his own music mere *entertainment* and claims to have built his success by strategically exploiting the music market: it is the clear awareness of a historical fact. And for the same reason Zappa can write, unintentionally recalling Adorno's concept of "decoration of empty time": "A composer's job involves *the decoration of fragments of time*. Without music to decorate it, time is just a bunch of boring *productive deadlines* or dates by which *bills must be paid*"[59]. The fact that the cultural industry can host its own radical self-denial is not due to its democratic transformation, but to the fact that it now completely dominates the horizon. Starting from this scenario, Zappa celebrates on one hand the definitive neutralization of avant-garde music, while, at the same time, allowing its most powerful and corrosive instincts to live a second life. This certainly has to do with the fact that his work enacts that complete emancipation of *amusement* that according to Adorno and Horkheimer "would be not only the opposite of art but its complementary extreme"[60].

It is obvious that Adorno's musicology could welcome Zappa as its immanent dialectical reversal only if we understand what Adorno calls "the temporal kernel of truth" (*Zeitkern*). Adorno's philosophy was centered on the concept of *Erfahrung*, on the idea that experience finds itself where subject and object meet, assuming that both subject and object are not steady and unchangeable poles. For this reason, my defense of pop music has started not from an alleged theoretical insufficiency of Adorno, but from a historical change in the object. If, as Hegel believed, "philosophy is its own time apprehended in thoughts", it should be clear why the undeniable historical limits of Adorno's thought

---

59 Zappa and Occhiogrosso 1989, p. 193.
60 GS 14, p. 164 (Adorno and Horkheimer 2002, p. 113).

become a sign of its truth: because a philosophy that has actually penetrated the essence of the historical movement that generates it, also captures the lines of flight that lead it beyond its historical horizon. The failure to understand where the chronicle of his days turned into history becomes a venial sin, if Adorno's work allows us to understand *a posteriori* what happened after his death in 1969. Indeed, the odd relationship between Adorno's musicology and the history of rock music seems to suggest that, sometimes, the same facts that prove us wrong, end up confirming our theory.

Bibliography

Adorno Th. W.
1970 ff. *Gesammelte Schriften* (quoted as GS) ed. by R. Tiedemann, Suhrkamp, Frankfurt a.M.
1976. *Introduction to the sociology of music*, trans. by E. B. Ashton, The Seabury Press, New York.
1994. "Vers une musique informelle", in *Quasi una Fantasia: Essays on Modern Music*, trans. by R. Livingstone, London-New York, Verso, pp. 269-322.
2001a. "On the Fetish-Character in Music and the Regression of Listening", in *The Culture Industry: Selected Essays on Mass Culture*, ed. by J. M. Bernstein, London, Routledge, pp. 29-60.
2001b. "The Schema of Mass Culture", in *The Culture Industry*, pp. 61-97.
2002a. "The Aging of the New Music", in *Essays on Music*, ed. by R. D. Leppert, trans. by S. H. Gillespie et al., Berkeley, University of California Press, pp. 181-202.
2002b. "Difficulties", in *Essays on Music*, pp. 644-680.
2003. "Zur Kulturindustrie" (quoted as ZK), Wiener Radio 21.2.1969, in *Adorno. Eine Bildmonographie*, Suhrkamp, Frankfurt a.M., pp. 288-290.
2006. *Current of Music. Elements of a Radio Theory* (quoted as CM), ed. by R. Hullot-Kentor, Suhrkamp, Frankfurt a.M.

Adorno Th. W. and Horkheimer M.
2002. *Dialectic of Enlightenment: Philosophical Fragments*, trans. by E. Jephcott, Stanford, Stanford University Press.

Buhler J.

2005. "Frankfurt School Blues: Rethinking Adorno's Critique of Jazz", in B. Hoeckner (ed.), *Apparitions. New Perspectives on Adorno and Twentieth-Century Music*, Routledge, New York, pp. 103-130.

Carboni M.
2012. "Introduction" to Th.W. Adorno, *Long Play e altri volteggi della puntina*, Castelvecchi, Roma.

Friedlander P.
1996. *Rock and Roll: A Social History*, Westview Press, Boulder.

Frith S.
1978. *The Sociology of Rock*. London, Constable and Comp. Limited.

Gracyk T.A.
1992. "Adorno, Jazz and the Aesthetics of Popular Music", in "The Musical Quarterly", vol. 76, n. 4, pp. 526-542.

Jenemann D.
2004. *Adorno in America*, University of Minnesota Press, Minneapolis.

Hullot-Kentor R.
2006. *Things Beyond Resemblance: Collected Essays on Theodor W. Adorno*, Columbia University Press, New York.

Levin Th. Y.
1990. "Adorno on Music in the Age of Its Technological Reproducibility", in "October", vol. 55, pp. 23-47.

Maurizi M.
2001. "No Foolin'. Dadaist strategies and instinct in Zappa and Beefheart" (1966-1970), in "Soundscapes", vol. 4, 2001 (available at: www.icce.rug.nl/~soundscapes/VOLUME04/No_foolin.shtml).
2018. *La vendetta di Dioniso. La musica contemporanea da Schönberg ai Nirvana*, Jaca Book, Milano.

McCartney P. et al.
1989. *The Paul McCartney World Tour*, Emap Metro – MPL, London.

Middleton R.
1990. *Studying Popular Music*, Open University Press, Milton Keynes & Philadelphia.

Paddison M.
1993. *Adorno's Aesthetics of Music*, Cambridge University Press, Cambridge.
1996. *Adorno, Modernism and Mass Culture*. Kahn and Averill, London.

Powell L.
2005. "Die Zerstörung der Symphonie": Adorno and the Theory of Radio", in B. Hoeckner (ed.), *Apparitions. New Perspectives on Adorno and Twentieth-Century Music*, Routledge, New York, pp. 131-150.

Santoro M.
2004. "Adorno e la sociologia critica della musica (*popular*)", Introduction to Th. W. Adorno, *Sulla popular music*, Armando, Roma.

Scherzinger M.
2005. "Music, Corporate Power, and the Age of Unending War", in B. Hoeckner (ed.), *Apparitions. New Perspectives on Adorno and Twentieth-Century Music*, Routledge, New York, pp. 151-182.

Schönherr U.
1991. "Adorno and Jazz: Reflections on a Failed Encounter", in "Telos", vol. 87, pp. 85-97.

Thomson A.
2006. *Adorno: A Guide for the Perplexed*, Continuum, London-New York.

Watson B.
1996. *Frank Zappa: The Negative Dialectic of Poodle Play*, St. Martin's Press, New York.

Witkin R. W.
1998. *Adorno on Music*, Routledge, New York.

Zappa F. and Occhiogrosso P.
1989. *The Real Frank Zappa Book*, Picador, London.

MIMESIS GROUP
www.mimesis-group.com

MIMESIS INTERNATIONAL
www.mimesisinternational.com
info@mimesisinternational.com

MIMESIS EDIZIONI
www.mimesisedizioni.it
mimesis@mimesisedizioni.it

ÉDITIONS MIMÉSIS
www.editionsmimesis.fr
info@editionsmimesis.fr

MIMESIS COMMUNICATION
www.mim-c.net

MIMESIS EU
www.mim-eu.com

Printed by
Geca Industrie Grafiche – San Giuliano Milanese (MI)
November 2019